Mark Carney Exposed

# Mark Carney Exposed

Elias Trent

# CONTENTS

ESG (Environmental, Social, and Governance):
A corporate scoring framework that measures a company's environmental sustainability, social responsibility, and internal governance practices. ESG is increasingly used to direct investment capital and influence corporate behavior—often criticized for being subjective, non-transparent, and politicized.

CBDC (Central Bank Digital Currency):
A state-backed digital version of a national currency issued by a central bank. Promoted as a secure, traceable, and programmable form of money, but widely criticized for enabling government surveillance, spending controls, and elimination of financial privacy.

WEF (World Economic Forum):
An international NGO headquartered in Switzerland, best known for its annual Davos summit. The WEF promotes global public-private cooperation and popularized terms like "The Great Reset" and "stakeholder capitalism." Frequently criticized for being an unelected influence hub of billionaires, bureaucrats, and technocrats.

Stakeholder Capitalism:
An economic model where corporations are accountable not just to shareholders, but to a broader range of "stakeholders"—including governments, NGOs, and civil society. Framed as more socially conscious than shareholder capitalism, but criticized for undermining property rights and democratic accountability.

Net-Zero Transition:
A global economic initiative aimed at reducing carbon emissions to net zero by 2050. Involves massive shifts in energy, finance, infrastructure, and agriculture. Promoted by Carney as the "greatest commercial opportunity of our time."

Carbon Credits:
Tradable certificates representing permission to emit a certain amount of carbon dioxide. Central to climate finance schemes, but heavily criticized for enabling greenwashing, speculation, and elite profit under the guise of environmentalism.

Green Bonds:
Debt instruments used to fund environmentally friendly projects. Considered part of the broader ESG investing strategy, but questions remain about transparency, efficacy, and actual environmental impact.

Technocracy:
A system of governance where decision-making is led by technical experts, bureaucrats, and economists rather than elected representatives. Promoted as efficient and evidence-based, but often seen as elitist, anti-democratic, and detached from public consent.

The Great Reset:
A post-COVID economic agenda launched by the WEF in 2020. Calls for "rebuilding better" through stakeholder capitalism, ESG, digital identity, and sustainable finance. Described by critics as a cover for technocratic overreach and economic centralization.

Privy Council (King's Privy Council for Canada):
A formal advisory body to the Canadian monarch, which in practice serves as a discretionary appointment list for high-level government advisors. Largely ceremonial today, but used to grant legal power and confidentiality to elite insiders—Carney among them.

Transition Finance:
Investments made to help companies shift from high-carbon to low-carbon operations. A core pillar of ESG and Carney's Brookfield portfolio, though often vague in scope and criticized for being little more than branding.

Climate Action and Finance (UN Special Envoy Role):
Carney's UN appointment to mobilize private capital toward climate goals. The position lacks direct accountability, and operates as a plat-

form to influence governments, central banks, and corporations in alignment with global ESG targets.

Digital Identity:

A digital representation of a person's verified attributes used to access services online and offline. Frequently discussed in tandem with CB-DCs and ESG to enable programmable rights, access, and permissions.

Mark Carney matters because he is the embodiment of the modern technocrat—unelected, unaccountable, and yet immensely powerful. To understand Carney is to understand how financial policy, global governance, and ideological rebranding converge into a new architecture of control. He is not just a banker. He is not just a bureaucrat. He is a front-facing symbol of a deeper, globalist infrastructure that has quietly replaced democratic will with corporate consensus.

His resume tells part of the story: Governor of the Bank of Canada. Governor of the Bank of England. Chair of the Financial Stability Board. Vice Chair and Head of ESG and Transition Investing at Brookfield Asset Management. And now, presumptive Prime Ministerial candidate for the Liberal Party of Canada. These roles are not the result of electoral approval, but selection by and for an inner circle of elites who control the flow of capital, the shape of climate policy, and the future of monetary sovereignty.

Carney's power is not confined to any one office. He is a node in a transnational network—a global finance priesthood that answers not to citizens, but to stakeholders, shareholders, and unelected panels. This is why he matters. Because he is not simply implementing policy; he is implementing ideology under the guise of inevitability. "Net Zero" is not a debate. ESG is not a choice. Digital currencies are not voted on. They are managed into existence, and Carney is among the chief managers.

He speaks the language of the reasonable man—of transition, resilience, and sustainability. But behind the euphemisms are policies that tighten the grip of banks over citizens, that elevate supranational institutions over national sovereignty, and that punish dissent through financial deplatforming and regulatory strangulation. When he warns of climate risk, what he really means is risk to the current financial architecture from any deviation from the plan.

Mark Carney does not sell policy—he sells inevitability. That's his greatest weapon. He packages technocracy as common sense, and wraps globalism in the flag of environmental virtue. When a man this powerful goes largely unchallenged—when no opposition party questions his proximity to the World Economic Forum, or his role in ESG-driven corporate monopolies—he becomes more than a public figure. He becomes a system unto himself.

Understanding Carney, then, is not optional. If Canadians wish to reclaim any semblance of democratic choice, of national direction, they must unmask those who lead by stealth and speak in the coded language of progress. Mark Carney is not just Canada's problem—he is the face of a broader global convergence between finance, governance, and ideology.

He matters not for who he is, but for what he represents.

There is no such thing as neutrality in finance or governance. The myth that technocrats like Mark Carney operate in an impartial, apolitical vacuum is one of the most dangerous illusions of our time. It is sold to the public through sterile language—"stability," "risk management," "transition frameworks," "macroeconomic tools"—that conceals what is really happening: ideological engineering via the balance sheet.

When Mark Carney speaks about inflation, climate change, or digital currencies, he is not offering neutral analysis. He is offering a worldview. A worldview in which democratic deliberation is subordinate to financial consensus. In which sovereign policy takes a backseat to global benchmarks. In which morality itself is measured in ESG scores and carbon credits. Finance is the new morality play, and Carney its soft-spoken high priest.

The myth of neutrality persists because institutions want it to. Central banks claim independence while shaping national destinies. Global finance firms push "green investing" while holding stakes in mining conglomerates, weapons manufacturers, and data surveillance firms.

Carney himself was Vice Chair at Brookfield, overseeing billions in energy assets, while simultaneously advocating for a net-zero transition—one he helped finance, regulate, and promote. Neutral?

No. Strategic.

The myth is effective because it disguises power. It suggests that policy is data-driven, not politically motivated. But there is always a choice in finance: what to subsidize, what to restrict, what to inflate, and what to let die. The printing of money is not neutral. It benefits some and burdens others. The introduction of carbon markets is not neutral. It shifts power from industry to bureaucracy. Central bank digital currencies are not neutral. They centralize surveillance and transaction control under the pretense of efficiency.

And so we return to the core danger of Carney's model: the pretense that technocracy is apolitical. In reality, it is deeply ideological—committed to stakeholder capitalism, elite consensus, and supranational governance. It undermines accountability while claiming moral high ground. It rewards conformity and punishes deviation.

By cloaking power in the language of science, economics, or climate urgency, Carney and his allies remove issues from the political arena and place them into managed frameworks—where no vote can reverse them, no referendum can challenge them, and no citizen can meaningfully opt out.

That's the myth. That's the game.

And until we expose it, the system will continue to move, not toward democracy or prosperity, but toward a managed decline dressed in the language of inevitable progress.

Technocracy is the new oligarchy—unaccountable, unelected, and masked in the language of expertise. Nowhere is this more evident than in the rise of ESG (Environmental, Social, and Governance) frameworks, a soft power mechanism dressed as a moral compass but functioning as a corporate straitjacket. And Mark Carney—former central banker turned ESG evangelist—is its most articulate apostle.

At first glance, ESG looks benign, even noble. Who wouldn't want cleaner air, better labor standards, and ethical boardrooms? But beneath the surface, ESG is a Trojan horse. It doesn't serve democracy. It sidesteps it. ESG metrics are not shaped by public vote or parliamentary debate. They are crafted by unelected advisory bodies, global consultancies, and asset managers with trillions under management. The public has no say. Yet these metrics now influence everything from pension funds to municipal investments. In effect, your economic future is being shaped not by your values, but by theirs.

Carney's transition from the Bank of England to Brookfield Asset Management, and from there to the UN and climate finance leadership, tells the story. He didn't retire into obscurity. He pivoted into global governance, leveraging his credibility to push ESG as the guiding rubric for future investment. At Brookfield, he oversaw billions in "green transition" portfolios while also holding major stakes in traditional infrastructure and fossil fuels. This is not ethical investing. It's financial colonialism cloaked in green.

ESG also rewards conformity. Corporations that toe the line—on climate, equity, or whatever the current value metric is—get access to cheaper credit, favorable media, and regulatory advantages. Those that don't are starved of capital or driven out of the market entirely. This isn't capitalism. It's behavioral engineering via financial leverage. It's not about creating value. It's about enforcing values—globalized, bureaucratized, and weaponized against dissent.

Technocracy and ESG together are the death knell of democratic accountability. Elected officials are increasingly irrelevant in the face of ratings agencies, central banks, and investment cartels. They don't legislate your future—they interpret mandates handed down by financial intermediaries. It's no wonder citizens feel powerless. Their vote can't compete with BlackRock's balance sheet or the IMF's conditionalities.

And this is by design. Carney has openly advocated for a "new financial system" where climate targets, inclusion goals, and global standards are "hardwired" into the economy. But who writes the code? Who audits the algorithm? Not you. Not me. Not anyone who can be removed from office. That's the fatal flaw of technocracy: it believes governance without consent is a virtue. That if only the right minds are in charge, the messy business of democracy can be replaced with spreadsheets and compliance departments.

But democracy is not a bug. It is the last firewall against totalizing control. ESG, in its current form, is not an expression of ethics. It is the erasure of accountability behind the façade of righteousness. And until we reclaim the economic levers from the technocrats who wield them, our future will not be governed—it will be programmed.

# Chapter 1: Prairie Grooming

Mark Carney's story begins far from the marble halls of central banks and global summits. He was born on March 16, 1965, in Fort Smith, Northwest Territories—a remote Canadian town nestled in the subarctic, where the northern lights hang low and winters are long. The son of a school principal and a teacher, Carney grew up in a household shaped by civic duty, education, and a strong sense of public responsibility. It was a setting that prized order, discipline, and achievement—but it also distanced him, both geographically and psychologically, from the populist pulse of Canada's cities.

Fort Smith is not the kind of place that grooms technocrats. It's rugged, isolated, and intimately aware of nature's unforgiving extremes. Yet it also sits at a crossroads between Indigenous territory, federal administration, and frontier pragmatism. These contrasts—between central authority and local reality, theory and lived experience—would follow Carney throughout his career, though he'd rarely acknowledge them.

The backdrop of his birth is important. Born just as Pierre Trudeau was rising to political power and recasting Canada as a centralized, multicultural state, Carney's early years unfolded in a country undergoing transformation—politically, economically, and socially. The quiet revolution in Quebec, the rise of federal power, and the emergence of technocratic liberalism would become the ideological terrain on which he built his identity.

Though Fort Smith is distant from the boardrooms of Toronto or the think tanks of London, Carney never forgot his origins—or at least, he never stopped invoking them. In interviews, he has spoken of growing up "with a strong sense of fairness," attributing it to his small-town upbringing. But whether that fairness was shaped by his environment or by the ambitions of a family committed to academic and social excellence is less clear. What is clear is this: from the start, Carney was not content to stay local. He was destined to leave Fort Smith behind—not in memory, but in practice.

His birth in the Canadian North serves today as a kind of mythic origin story—a populist flourish used to soften the sharper edges of his elite career. But it is just that: a story. The real Carney is not a product of Fort Smith. He is a creation of global finance, Ivy League institutions, and transnational governance. His life in the Northwest Territories was not the soil from which his ideas grew. It was the point of departure.

Mark Carney's educational path reads like a blueprint for technocratic ascent. After leaving the small-town confines of Fort Smith and graduating high school in Edmonton, he entered the Ivy League world of Harvard University—where his credentials would be stamped with elite approval. There, Carney studied economics and graduated in 1988 with a bachelor's degree that reflected more than just academic achievement: it marked his entry into a transnational class of thinkers and policymakers who would soon reshape the post-Cold War global order.

At Harvard, Carney absorbed the prevailing neoliberal orthodoxy of the 1980s. This was the era of Reagan and Thatcher, of deregulation, globalization, and market worship disguised as freedom. The Department of Economics at Harvard was a training ground for future central bankers, IMF officials, and investment strategists—individuals groomed not to question the system, but to manage it more efficiently. In this environment, Carney learned that markets were not to be restrained by national sovereignty, but rather optimized by data, algorithms, and "informed" policy choices. Democracy was an afterthought. Efficiency was king.

He didn't stop there.

Carney secured a Rhodes Scholarship to Oxford University, where he earned a master's degree and later a doctorate in economics at St. Peter's College. His time at Oxford further solidified his credentials—not merely in economic theory, but in the unspoken codes of the global elite. Oxford was not just about scholarship; it was about network, perception, polish. A man who could move seamlessly between Harvard's technocratic pragmatism and Oxford's philosophical gravitas would be well-positioned to rule without ever having to run.

His doctoral thesis—focused on the dynamics of exchange rates and inflation in emerging markets—offered an early glimpse into the world he would one day dominate. But it also revealed something deeper: Carney's instinct to abstract complex human economies into impersonal models. Like many of his generation, he was trained to see economies not as collections of people with moral agency, but as systems to be optimized and managed.

What he lacked in ideological boldness, he made up for in institutional fluency. Carney emerged from Oxford as the perfect technocrat: intelligent without being visionary, adaptable without being unpredictable, and most of all, credible to the powerful.

His education was not about cultivating originality—it was about earning trust from the global ruling class. And in that, he succeeded brilliantly.

Mark Carney's early life doesn't offer the tale of a visionary outsider rising from obscurity—it reflects something subtler, and far more common in today's managerial elite: an early absorption of establishment values disguised as personal ambition.

Born in Fort Smith, Northwest Territories, and raised in Edmonton, Alberta, Carney's upbringing was modest but hardly detached from professional ambition. His father was a high school principal turned academic, and his mother was a school teacher—both firmly embedded in the Canadian public education system. These were people who believed in the system, and who raised a son to rise through it, not against it. There was no radical edge, no real rebellion—just a quiet, disciplined trajectory of achievement.

From an early age, Carney stood out not because of grand dreams, but because of his adaptability and his knack for aligning with the expectations of authority figures. He wasn't a disrupter; he was a student of systems. He didn't challenge structures—he excelled within them. This became a pattern: he learned how to fit the mold better than most, and he was rewarded for it.

There's no clear evidence of grand ideological conviction in Carney's youth—no early declarations about reshaping the world or fighting injustice. If anything, his ambitions were shaped by a refined version of Canadian pragmatism: do well, keep your head down, and rise. The son of two educators, he adopted the value of performance, of doing what was expected and doing it better than anyone else.

But here's the rub—those values, when fused with elite education, produced something more than just a high-achiever. They produced a man capable of operating in the upper echelons of finance and politics without ever appearing political. His early ambition was not to change the world, but to navigate it, to master its levers and institutions. And by mastering them, he would eventually help redefine them—quietly, efficiently, and always under the banner of neutrality.

Carney's values were not radical. They were bureaucratic excellence, elite competence, and managerial confidence. But in today's global order, that's more than enough to shape nations.

# Chapter 2: Goldman Sachs | Making a Globalist

If Mark Carney's academic journey provided the credentials, his thirteen-year tenure at Goldman Sachs forged the worldview. Goldman was more than just a training ground—it was a baptism into the highest tier of global finance, a place where loyalty to the firm blurred into loyalty to a transnational elite. This was where Carney became fluent in the language of capital—not as an abstract force, but as the mechanism that runs the world.

At Goldman, Carney wasn't pushing paper. He was deep in the engine room, working in sovereign risk and managing debt portfolios for nations, not just corporations. His resume includes time in London, New York, Tokyo, and Toronto—strategically rotating through the major financial capitals of the globe. This wasn't just about learning markets; it was about learning how to think beyond borders. National economies became spreadsheets. Governments became clients. Everything could be priced, hedged, and, if necessary, leveraged.

He didn't just observe the global order from the outside—he learned to manage its machinery from within. And crucially, Goldman taught him the ultimate lesson of modern finance: power is not held by those who make laws, but by those who shape liquidity. This was Carney's initiation into the quiet corridors of influence, where supranational organizations, multinational banks, and elite think tanks set the agenda far removed from democratic scrutiny.

Goldman Sachs was infamous, even then, for its alumni network—a pipeline that feeds directly into central banks, treasuries, and supranational institutions like the IMF and World Bank. Carney's entry into that ecosystem wasn't accidental. He was the perfect fit: articulate, competent, ideologically malleable. He wasn't radical, but he was ambitious. Not confrontational, but calculating. In the world of high finance, that made him dangerous.

By the time he left Goldman in 2003, Carney had been shaped into something more than a banker. He had absorbed a creed: that markets must be managed, that risk must be socialized, and that governance should be guided by technocrats rather than voters. Goldman taught him not just how money moves—but how power conceals itself within the movement of money.

It is no coincidence that so many "public servants" today pass through Goldman's halls. It is not a bank; it is a proving ground for the globalist class. Carney emerged from it as a man who could operate as a central banker, a climate czar, or a policy whisperer. He left Goldman with a Rolodex of sovereign leaders and a worldview that sees democracy as inefficient and public consent as an afterthought.

This was the crucible. This is where the mask of Canadian modesty fused with the machinery of international control. And it's where Mark Carney—the globalist technocrat—was born.

To understand the reach of Mark Carney, one must first understand the revolving door—Goldman Sachs' signature contribution to modern governance. It's a model of seamless integration between private finance and public policy, where former investment bankers become central bank governors, treasury secretaries, and climate envoys without ever changing loyalties. Goldman Sachs doesn't just produce financiers. It manufactures influence. And Carney is a near-perfect embodiment of this model.

The so-called "alumni club" of Goldman Sachs is not some symbolic designation. It is an operational network—tightly wound, discreet, and extraordinarily effective. Its members pass from one role to another with uncanny ease, occupying the most sensitive and powerful positions in the financial and political architecture of the modern world. And while their job titles may change—CEO, central banker, climate envoy, or finance minister—their ideological commitments and class alliances remain disturbingly consistent.

When Carney left Goldman in 2003, he didn't leave the club—he simply took on a new role in a new wing of the same establishment. He stepped into the Canadian Department of Finance, later moving on to the Bank of Canada, and eventually the Bank of England. At each stop, he implemented policies that aligned more with market logic than democratic accountability. Inflation targeting, austerity-friendly rate regimes, and bailouts disguised as stability—all executed with the quiet assurance of someone who knew he would never be held to account by the voting public.

And it's not just Carney. The Goldman pipeline runs deep. Consider Mario Draghi—former Goldman executive turned European Central Bank president. Or Robert Rubin—Goldman co-chairman turned U.S. Treasury Secretary. Or Hank Paulson, who did the same and handed out trillion-dollar bailouts during the 2008 crash to protect the very institutions he once ran. The same doors swing open for them all. Public office is simply the next boardroom.

This revolving door doesn't just blur the lines between public and private—it erases them. When the same people rotate between roles, institutions become indistinguishable. Is the Bank of England a public body or a Goldman satellite office? Is the UN's climate finance initiative serving global interests or multinational capital? When Mark Carney becomes Chair of Brookfield Asset Management, then the UN climate envoy, and now a potential prime ministerial candidate, does he represent the people—or his peers in the alumni club?

Carney's trajectory is not exceptional. It is prototypical. He is what Goldman alumni are trained to become: highly literate in financial complexity, ideologically loyal to market technocracy, and entirely detached from the consequences of their decisions. The revolving door works because those who pass through it understand their real constituency is not voters or citizens—it is capital itself.

And here lies the central danger: democratic institutions, already fragile, are being gradually replaced by transnational networks of unelected elites. The Goldman alumni club is not just a symptom of this trend—it is its architect. Through this revolving door, global policy is engineered not in parliaments, but in boardrooms. And Mark Carney walks through it smiling—untouched, unaccountable, and ever upward.

### The Beginning of a Career of Quiet Consolidation

Mark Carney's ascent into the halls of power was never marked by bombast or radical declarations. It was, instead, defined by precision, discipline, and a remarkable ability to operate within the machinery of existing institutions while subtly tightening their alignment with a technocratic, finance-first worldview. This was not a man who sought change from the outside—Carney's genius lay in infiltrating the system from within, and then recalibrating it with surgical efficiency. His was a career of quiet consolidation: consolidating power, influence, and institutional trust under the guise of competent stewardship.

From his early days at the Department of Finance in Canada, Carney made it clear that his strengths lay in policy fluency and bureaucratic navigation. He didn't bring populist rhetoric or big promises; he brought models, numbers, and a Harvard-educated fluency in elite code-switching. While most Canadians couldn't have picked him out of a lineup, Bay Street and Ottawa insiders recognized in him a valuable asset—a man who could make the interests of finance appear as public goods.

His rapid rise to the Governorship of the Bank of Canada in 2008 was no accident. Behind the scenes, Carney had already begun crafting a profile that bridged credibility with discretion. He didn't court headlines; he secured confidence. The financial crisis gave him the perfect backdrop. Canada emerged from the 2008 meltdown relatively unscathed, and Carney was positioned as the prudent guardian of Canadian economic stability. What few noticed was the ideological underpinning of that "stability"—policies that prioritized asset inflation, capital consolidation, and monetary insulation of the banking elite.

This phase of his career wasn't about front-facing influence—it was about building institutional power. Carney deepened the authority of central banking, not as a democratic safeguard, but as an autonomous technocracy—beyond political reach and shielded from public pressure. At the Bank of Canada, and later at the Bank of England, he nurtured a new orthodoxy: one in which monetary policy served as a political tool masquerading as neutral science. His consolidation of credibility gave cover to an expansion of influence, and that influence was directed not toward rebalancing the system, but reinforcing its most extractive structures.

At each level of Carney's ascent, the same pattern emerged: avoid scrutiny, deepen control. He was the architect of "forward guidance," a term that sounds benign but in practice meant long-term guarantees to capital markets that the central bank would act in their favor. He institutionalized complex communication strategies that made central banking even more opaque to the public. And perhaps most significantly, he helped usher in the era of ESG—environmental, social, and governance-based investing—as a new frontier for capital, further tightening finance's grip on every sphere of public and private life.

In retrospect, this was the period where the future of governance was quietly rewritten. Under Carney's leadership, central banks ceased to be merely monetary institutions—they became cultural authorities, climate advisors, and social arbiters. None of this was framed as revolution. It was presented as prudence. And therein lies Carney's greatest strength: the ability to radically reshape institutions under the polite cloak of moderation.

His was not a populist rise. It was a coronation by committee. A career crafted not in the daylight of public discourse, but in the airless rooms of policy briefings, economic forums, and Davos salons. It is here, away from voters, that Carney consolidated not only his power—but the very template of twenty-first-century governance: post-democratic, market-led, and impeccably credentialed.

The quiet consolidation continues. And Carney, ever the polished technocrat, remains the high priest of this new order.

3

# Chapter 3: Canada's Banker, but Whose Interests?

Mark Carney's appointment as Governor of the Bank of Canada in 2008 was heralded as a triumph of meritocracy and global savvy. The headlines praised his fluency in markets, his Harvard and Oxford pedigree, and his credibility with international finance. At a time when global institutions were losing legitimacy, Carney was cast as the face of calm and competence. But beneath the applause and accolades, a deeper question lingered—who, exactly, was Carney serving? And what vision of Canada did his policies reflect?

Carney assumed control of Canada's central bank at a pivotal moment. The global financial system was in a state of near-collapse. American and European banks were buckling under the weight of bad loans, derivatives, and decades of unregulated speculation. In Canada, the crisis was milder—but only because of previous regulatory inertia, not foresight. The big banks weren't saved by policy genius; they had simply never fully adopted the toxic assets poisoning Wall Street. Carney was handed a stable system and lionized for keeping it that way. The myth of his genius was seeded early and grew quickly.

But governance is not judged solely by what is prevented. It must also be measured by what is promoted. And Carney's reign at the Bank of Canada was marked by an aggressive expansion of monetary policy tools that deepened structural inequalities while masquerading as economic stewardship. He ushered in ultra-low interest rates, flooding the system with cheap money in the name of stimulus. This enriched asset holders—banks, corporations, and homeowners in hot markets—while leaving wage-earners and renters behind. The result? A massive, artificial inflation of housing prices and an unsustainable credit bubble that would come to define a generation of indebted Canadians.

Under Carney's watch, the Bank of Canada became more politicized—not by engaging in partisan fights, but by pursuing a policy agenda rooted in an unspoken ideology: technocratic capitalism. The Bank acted as if it were above politics, when in reality it was reinforcing one side of the economic spectrum—protecting capital at all costs while letting productivity, innovation, and wages stagnate. It began issuing forward guidance that all but guaranteed stability for investors, creating a sense of certainty for the financial elite that the central bank would always have their back.

What went unnoticed by most Canadians was how closely Carney's policies aligned with global financial interests. His relationships with the IMF, the World Economic Forum, and other elite institutions weren't just ceremonial. He was an active participant in shaping the global consensus around inflation targets, risk management, and financial regulation—not as a defender of Canadian sovereignty, but as a broker of consensus among unelected power centers. The interests of Main Street were never his priority. His concern was confidence—in markets, in liquidity, in global financial flows. Canada's working class? A rounding error in spreadsheets.

He also began laying the ideological groundwork for ESG finance—the seed of his later career. During his tenure, Carney made early overtures toward incorporating climate risk into financial modeling. On the surface, this sounded progressive. But ESG as Carney envisioned it was not about environmental justice or sustainability. It was about commodifying concern, turning social and climate issues into new metrics for investment risk—thereby creating an entirely new market for technocratic management. Green bonds, climate disclosures, and impact indexes weren't designed to protect the planet. They were designed to create new instruments for profit and new forms of regulatory capture.

Carney's Bank of Canada didn't democratize finance. It mystified it. It did not bring transparency. It institutionalized opacity. Under his leadership, central banking took on the appearance of priesthood—delivering oracles in coded language, guarded by jargon and inaccessibility. The ordinary citizen could no longer discern where the economy ended and ideology began.

This chapter of Carney's career is best understood as a dress rehearsal for global power. He learned how to govern a nation without ever facing its electorate. He perfected the art of speaking in platitudes while executing precision strategies for capital preservation. He crafted the illusion of neutrality while presiding over one of the most lopsided wealth transfers in modern Canadian history.

He was Canada's banker, yes. But whose ledger was he really balancing? And who, in the end, was left to pay the interest?

The answer, as always with technocrats, is buried in policy frameworks, rate announcements, and spreadsheet assumptions—hidden from democratic review, but felt acutely in every paycheck that couldn't cover the rent, in every young Canadian priced out of their own economy. That's the legacy of Carney's Canada.

## Monetary Policy During the 2008 Crash—and Taking False Credit for the Work of Jim Flaherty

The 2008 financial crisis marked a pivotal test for economic leadership around the world. Central banks scrambled to prop up collapsing financial systems. Governments injected capital to prevent full-blown depression. In Canada, however, a different narrative quickly emerged—one that painted the country as a beacon of fiscal stability, sound banking, and prudent leadership. And central to that story, at least in the public imagination, was Mark Carney.

He was the face on magazine covers. The man of the hour at global summits. The "rock star" central banker who, according to fawning headlines, saved Canada from the economic inferno that consumed much of the developed world. But the story wasn't true. At least, not in the way it was told.

The real architect of Canada's economic response was not Carney—it was Finance Minister Jim Flaherty.

While Carney was the public-facing central banker, it was Flaherty's policies—quietly, deliberately executed—that actually positioned Canada to weather the storm better than most. The key facts are clear: Canada's banks were already more conservative than their American counterparts, not because of Carney's oversight, but because of legislation introduced years earlier that prevented the kind of reckless subprime lending that had become the norm in the U.S.

In fact, during his time at Goldman Sachs, Carney had championed many of the same deregulatory attitudes that had led to the collapse abroad. He was no Cassandra predicting doom. When the crisis hit, his solution—like every other central banker—was to slash interest rates to near-zero and inject liquidity into the system. It was the standard central bank playbook, not an act of genius. But the myth of his economic foresight persisted, largely because he spoke the fluent dialect of elite financial circles and offered a comforting figure for markets desperate for certainty.

Meanwhile, Flaherty, working through the Department of Finance, implemented a stimulus package and bank backstops that kept liquidity flowing through the real economy—without the kind of bloated bailouts seen in the U.S. He moved quickly to secure mortgage lending through the Canada Mortgage and Housing Corporation (CMHC), helping maintain confidence in housing markets. He protected depositors, not just investors. And crucially, he resisted pressures to emulate Wall Street's excesses in the first place.

Carney's role, by contrast, was reactive, not revolutionary. He followed the lead of the U.S. Federal Reserve in slashing the overnight rate. He took credit for Canada's relative banking strength, which had nothing to do with his policies and everything to do with regulatory frameworks already in place before his appointment.

Worse still, Carney became a master of narrative capture. The press—ever eager for a charismatic technocrat—latched onto his photogenic persona and Ivy League résumé. He was praised for his calm demeanor during parliamentary testimony, his global polish, and his capacity to "reassure markets." But these were rhetorical skills, not economic innovations. The central bank did not create stability—it projected the illusion of stability, while Canada's actual stability was due to policy groundwork laid by a government often at odds with Carney's worldview.

In private, Carney was known to dismiss Flaherty's fiscal conservatism as politically inconvenient. Yet it was precisely that conservatism—a refusal to follow Europe into fiscal oblivion—that protected Canada from the worst of the damage. Carney got the spotlight. Flaherty bore the responsibility.

And then there's the ethical question: Did Carney ever correct the record? Did he ever step forward to acknowledge that the so-called "Canadian miracle" was a team effort—and that the decisive moves were made not by the Bank, but by elected officials? No. He allowed the myth to grow. He benefitted from it. He parlayed it into global prestige and international appointments, eventually riding it all the way to the Bank of England and then into the ESG elite class.

This wasn't humility—it was branding. And the cost of that branding is still being paid. Canadians today live under the weight of policy inertia built on the false narrative of a central bank savior. Meanwhile, the public remains misled about how crises are truly averted: not by speeches, but by hard policy choices made outside the media glare.

Jim Flaherty, by all fair accounts, should be remembered as the man who actually stabilized Canada's economy in 2008. Carney, on the other hand, proved to be what technocrats often are: good at taking credit, poor at accountability.

History, if it's written honestly, will set the record straight. But the danger of false messiahs in modern finance is that they don't just rewrite the past—they shape the future. And as Carney now positions himself for political power, it's worth remembering just how much of his reputation was built on the work of others.

### First Signals of Carney's Ideological Ambitions

Mark Carney's early tenure as a central banker was draped in the garb of impartiality—steady hand, neutral expert, technocrat above politics. But beneath the public veneer of fiscal orthodoxy, there were signs—subtle at first, then unmistakable—that Carney's ambitions extended beyond monetary policy and into the ideological architecture of global governance.

The first real signal came not from what he did in the Bank of Canada's boardroom, but from how he spoke in international forums. Carney began using the language of transformation—not in terms of economic cycles or inflation targets, but in reference to "inclusive capitalism," "net-zero economies," and "global transition frameworks." These weren't the words of a banker stewarding interest rates. These were the talking points of someone positioning himself as a philosopher-king of finance, guiding not just markets but morals.

Even before he left Canada, Carney was already framing central banking as a lever for reshaping society. At G20 summits and World Economic Forum panels, he hinted that monetary authorities should play a role in managing climate change, inequality, and financial inclusivity. The problem? None of those mandates had been granted by any electorate. They were assumed—self-appointed missions under the guise of financial stewardship.

This pivot from practical economist to global ideologue became more apparent in speeches like his 2013 address at Osgoode Hall, where he spoke of the need for "true capitalism" to be "inclusive," "long-term," and "sustainable." He criticized the culture of short-term profit-seeking—a strange irony coming from a Goldman Sachs alumnus who had, for over a decade, profited from precisely that model. But this wasn't about consistency. It was about positioning. Carney was already crafting the narrative of a new kind of central banker—part financier, part climate warrior, part high priest of stakeholder economics.

And behind the rhetoric, the apparatus was quietly forming.

During his final years at the Bank of Canada, Carney became an early proponent of what would become ESG (Environmental, Social, Governance) metrics as a framework for systemic risk management. He began pushing the idea that climate change posed a "material financial risk" and therefore had to be priced into lending and insurance markets. This wasn't just climate awareness. It was the beginning of a technocratic justification for embedding climate ideology directly into capital allocation decisions, via institutions unelected and unaccountable to the public.

The implications were enormous—and deliberate. If climate policy could be framed as a financial risk, then central banks, pension funds, and investment managers could become the new enforcement wing of environmental policy—without a single vote cast. Carney was one of the first high-level financial figures to realize this. And rather than wait for political consensus, he began building the framework quietly from inside the house.

When he transitioned to the Bank of England in 2013, the messaging became more explicit. There, in the financial heart of the Commonwealth, he used his perch not just to steer interest rates, but to reshape global capitalism itself. The softly spoken Canadian central banker was transforming into something else entirely: a policy entrepreneur with a mission.

He began co-chairing panels on climate finance. He collaborated with global NGOs and think tanks to define metrics for "sustainable investment." He promoted the Task Force on Climate-related Financial Disclosures (TCFD), an initiative that would eventually become a regulatory blueprint for climate compliance through financial markets. This was not apolitical. It was, in fact, the birth of a new ideology—one that sought to centralize decision-making about global transitions in the hands of financial elites, under the camouflage of risk mitigation.

Carney's ideological ambitions can be summed up this way: he believed markets could be used to enforce moral outcomes, bypassing political debate, democratic contestation, and even constitutional limits.

He wasn't alone in this belief, but he was one of the first to turn it into a cohesive strategy. The central bank would no longer just control inflation—it would redirect the flow of capital based on an elite consensus of what the future should look like.

In retrospect, the signs were all there. A banker who spoke like a regulator. A regulator who thought like an activist. A technocrat who moved like a globalist. And through it all, a man who never once stood for election, yet whose influence grew steadily over the very mechanisms that underpin democratic societies.

Carney didn't just want to interpret the world—he wanted to remake it. The only question that remained was whether he would do so from behind the curtain of central banking or step into the political spotlight himself.

We now know the answer.

# Chapter 4: London Calling – The Bank of England

When Mark Carney was appointed Governor of the Bank of England in 2012, it raised eyebrows across the financial and political spectrum. A Canadian—a foreigner—at the helm of the world's second-oldest central bank? It was an unprecedented move. But it was also a message, one that signaled a shift not only in how the City of London saw its role in the world, but in how global finance was being quietly restructured into a supranational system managed by a class of unelected technocrats.

Carney was no ordinary Canadian. By then, he had become the financial world's golden boy. His time at the Bank of Canada had been framed as a masterclass in crisis management. He had weathered the 2008 financial storm with apparent calm and decisiveness—never mind that much of the heavy lifting was done by Jim Flaherty and the more conservative nature of Canada's banking system itself. Still, Carney's carefully cultivated image as the "steady hand in a storm" made him a darling of global financial institutions and policy elites alike.

The British establishment, reeling from its own failures during the crash, needed a reset. The Bank of England was about to receive unprecedented new powers—including macroprudential oversight of the entire financial system—and it needed someone with both credibility and ideological alignment to lead the transition. Carney checked every box. He had the right pedigree (Harvard and Oxford), the right network

(Goldman Sachs, G30, WEF), and most importantly, the right world-view. He believed that markets could be guided—not left alone—and that central banks should lead the moral transformation of capitalism.

In many ways, Carney wasn't chosen in spite of being Canadian. He was chosen because of it. As an outsider, he came without the baggage of the British financial caste system. He wasn't beholden to the old boys' clubs of Eton or Cambridge. That gave him the appearance of neutrality—but only the appearance. In reality, Carney represented something more radical than any hereditary lord or public school banker: the arrival of a transnational managerial elite who moved between continents, institutions, and mandates with seamless impunity.

He arrived at Threadneedle Street with a mandate far beyond monetary policy. His real job was to shepherd the integration of British finance into a new global order—one shaped not by voters, but by regulators, bankers, and NGOs under the banner of "resilience," "sustainability," and "transition." The financial elite of London didn't need another traditionalist. They needed a man of the new era: fluent in ESG, loyal to Davos, and armed with the credibility of technocratic "success." Carney was the perfect cipher.

Behind the scenes, Carney was already being groomed for this elevation. His move was orchestrated not by chance but by invitation—courted by George Osborne, Britain's Chancellor of the Exchequer at the time, who saw in Carney a globalist partner who could rebrand the reputation of the Bank and help position London as a leader in post-crash reform. The fact that Carney would become the first non-British governor in the Bank's 319-year history was portrayed as a strength. He was the outsider who would fix the insiders' mess.

But fix is a generous term. Carney didn't come to clean house—he came to rebuild the architecture of financial control on a different foundation. Under his leadership, the Bank of England pivoted from inflation-targeting to "mission-oriented finance." He began linking climate risk to financial stability, launched working groups on the greening of capital, and continued pushing ESG and net-zero frameworks through every regulatory channel available. This wasn't policy evolution. This was an ideological transformation of the institution's very soul.

In public, he maintained the tone of the dispassionate expert. But behind closed doors, Carney was reshaping the rules. He encouraged the Financial Stability Board, which he chaired, to develop climate-related disclosure standards. He backed central bank coordination on climate initiatives, knowing full well that these initiatives would soon become de facto global policy, even if no one had ever voted for them. He advocated for corporate governance reform under the banner of "stakeholder capitalism"—a model in which managers and activists, not shareholders or citizens, held the reins.

And London—already drifting from its national moorings—was the perfect laboratory.

In truth, Carney's Bank of England tenure wasn't about the pound or domestic policy. It was about proving that financial governance could become global governance, and that the central banker of the future would be more than a steward of currency. He would be a moral authority, a sustainability czar, and a partner to global NGOs and corporate coalitions. The real revolution wasn't monetary. It was ideological.

So why was a Canadian chosen to run Britain's central bank?

Because the institution no longer saw itself as purely British.

Because the new role of central banking was no longer neutral.

And because Mark Carney was already fluent in the language of global control.

His Influence Over Brexit-Era Financial Policy

As the United Kingdom lurched toward its eventual departure from the European Union, one figure emerged not as an elected leader, but as a kind of economic high priest presiding over the unraveling of a political era: Mark Carney.

Though nominally neutral and supposedly apolitical, Carney leveraged his position as Governor of the Bank of England to shape the financial narrative of Brexit in ways that were anything but impartial. He became a vocal participant in what many dubbed "Project Fear"—a coordinated effort among government institutions, financial analysts, and media elites to dissuade the British public from supporting Leave by forecasting economic apocalypse. Carney's Bank issued dire warnings: house prices could plummet, unemployment could soar, and the financial system could destabilize.

Yet none of this came to pass.

That didn't stop Carney from using his pulpit to amplify the risks, exaggerate the unknowns, and nudge the debate toward supranational 'solutions.' In so doing, he not only cemented his image as a guardian of orthodoxy, but also revealed his deeper ideological orientation: Carney believed in a tightly integrated, centrally managed global economy, not in the messy realities of national sovereignty.

In an age of democratic turbulence, he spoke the language of institutional continuity. And he made it clear that Brexit was not only economically inefficient, but morally and philosophically misaligned with the new world order he and his peers envisioned. His primary concern wasn't the will of the people—it was the stability of markets, and more precisely, the stability of the rules-based international financial order in which technocrats like himself held the keys.

Under his watch, the Bank of England used the uncertainty of Brexit to justify increasing its own discretionary power. Forward guidance became less about inflation targets and more about preserving "confidence." The Bank dipped into uncharted waters of financial contingency planning, crafting crisis scenarios that were less about probability than psychological persuasion. Leaked memos, "no-deal" forecasts, and shadow briefings to journalists—these weren't accidents. They were strategy.

Carney also played a behind-the-scenes role in ensuring that London's financial district—The City—remained as insulated as possible from the political fallout of Brexit. While manufacturing and agriculture were often left to twist in the wind, the financial sector benefited from carefully negotiated regulatory accommodations. Carney's message to global capital was simple: whatever happens with the populists, The City is still open for business.

He cultivated a vision of the post-Brexit UK that had less to do with democratic renewal and more to do with becoming a hub for green finance, global insurance markets, and climate-risk derivatives—a vision firmly embedded in his broader ESG framework. In essence, Carney offered Brexit Britain not freedom, but a different kind of subservience—to the climate agenda, to technocratic consensus, to corporate governance managed through environmental and social metrics.

Many assumed that Carney, as a Canadian and an outsider, would remain neutral in the debate. But this assumption misunderstood the deeper game. Carney was not loyal to Britain, nor to Canada, nor to any nation-state in the traditional sense. He was—and remains—an operator for a post-national ideology, one that sees politics as a risk factor to be managed and democracy as a cost center to be trimmed.

Brexit posed a threat not because it might trigger short-term volatility, but because it asserted the primacy of national will over transnational order. It reminded Carney and his cohort that people might still want to govern themselves, even if that meant leaving behind the soft tyranny of regulatory interdependence.

In his final years at the Bank of England, Carney shifted toward legacy building, embedding climate mandates and social responsibility metrics into institutional frameworks so that his vision would endure long after his departure. Brexit may have removed Britain from the EU, but Carney's mission was to ensure that it never left the ideological orbit of global finance.

And in that, he was largely successful.

## The Rise of Carney as a Media-Savvy Elite

Mark Carney's ascent was not merely a tale of monetary policy, institutional reform, or international finance—it was, perhaps most importantly, a carefully managed narrative. If his economic decisions built the scaffolding of his career, it was his public image that cemented his position as one of the most trusted and well-polished members of the global elite.

Unlike the gray men of central banking past, Carney understood early that power in the 21st century required not just competence, but brand. And Carney, with his clean-cut Harvard polish, Oxford intellect, and calm demeanor, offered the perfect character to play the new role of public-facing technocrat. He was the reassuring father figure, the rational mind in an irrational world, the fluent spokesman for a financial order slowly detaching from democratic oversight.

He gave media what it wanted: soundbites for stability, calm amid crisis, and just enough moral gravitas to make global finance feel like it had a soul.

His speeches were not dry central bank briefings. They were crafted performances—peppered with references to climate change, social justice, and inclusive growth. Carney learned to speak activist while governing like a banker. He regularly appeared at World Economic Forum panels, BBC interviews, and op-eds in elite papers with headlines like "Capitalism is Failing. Here's How to Fix It". And despite representing one of the most powerful institutions in the world, he was rarely met with criticism—only praise for his "vision" and "courage."

In reality, Carney was doing what technocrats had always done—but now cloaked in a progressive, media-friendly language that disarmed scrutiny. He didn't just raise interest rates or adjust inflation targets. He crafted narratives about systemic risk, green transitions, and sustainable capitalism—and he did it with camera-ready poise.

This media strategy wasn't an accident.

Carney surrounded himself with communication experts, worked closely with public relations strategists, and curated his every move with attention to optics. From carefully staged "town halls" to TED-style speaking engagements, he increasingly positioned himself as a thought leader, not just a banker. In a world where perception is influence, Carney mastered the art of authority through visibility. He became a mainstay of the Davos circuit—not just attending, but often chairing sessions and shaping outcomes behind closed doors.

In many ways, he became the prototype for a new kind of global elite: post-national, media-literate, ideologically aligned, and cloaked in the language of reform while consolidating control. He was the technocrat as influencer, fluent not only in the models of macroeconomics, but in the optics of power.

It's worth asking: when was the last time a central banker was profiled glowingly in Vanity Fair?

Or offered a leadership position with the United Nations on climate finance?

Or proposed as a future Prime Minister without ever standing for election?

These weren't fringe ideas. They were floated seriously in major publications and discussed openly in political circles. Because Carney wasn't just being managed by the media. He was managing it—using its tools to project calm competence, to sell global coordination as moral necessity, and to blur the line between expert and messiah.

Through this transformation, Carney's real talent emerged: not as a financial innovator, but as a legitimizer of global technocracy. He gave the public a palatable version of elite control, one dressed in the language of responsibility and equity. But behind the curtain, he was always executing the same mission: centralizing power, depoliticizing decisions, and embedding finance deeper into the cultural and political institutions of everyday life.

In short, Carney didn't just ride the rise of globalism—he became its public face.

A man not elected, but celebrated.

Not held accountable, but trusted implicitly.

Not because of what he did—but because of how well he played the part.

# Chapter 5: Green Is the New Gold

Mark Carney's transition from central banker to private sector executive was hardly a retreat—it was a coronation. In 2020, Carney accepted the role of Vice Chair at Brookfield Asset Management, one of the largest alternative investment firms on the planet, overseeing nearly a trillion dollars in assets. The man once hailed as the world's most trusted central banker had officially crossed over into the world of profit—albeit under the banner of public good.

But Carney wasn't just a Vice Chair. He was appointed Head of ESG and Impact Investing—a role so perfectly tailored to his new public persona that it almost seemed fictional. This wasn't a coincidence. ESG—Environmental, Social, and Governance—had become the new frontier of global finance, and Carney had positioned himself at its helm.

He claimed to be reinventing capitalism. In reality, he was repackaging the same structures of elite control under a fresh coat of green paint.

Under Carney's watch, ESG went from a niche set of investment criteria to a worldwide moral imperative. He didn't merely advocate for green finance; he attempted to create the rules that defined it. Through the Task Force on Climate-related Financial Disclosures (TCFD) and his central role at COP26, Carney helped establish the frameworks that would determine which companies were deemed "sustainable" enough to qualify for trillions in investment capital.

This was no small thing.

It meant governments, central banks, and pension funds could now be pressured to divest from anything non-compliant with ESG goals. And who got to define those goals? Increasingly—Carney. Or, more precisely, Carney and the network of unelected technocrats, institutional investors, and multinational boardrooms that surrounded him.

Meanwhile, Brookfield stood to benefit enormously. One of the world's largest infrastructure and real estate players, Brookfield was already moving aggressively into "transition investing"—buying up utilities, green energy projects, and carbon offset markets. ESG wasn't a movement to them—it was a business model.

Carney was both the architect and the beneficiary.

While in his public role he continued to champion net-zero, green growth, and sustainable capitalism, in private he oversaw the redirection of enormous financial flows into Brookfield-linked ventures. All while maintaining the public image of a man above reproach.

This was the quiet financialization of morality—the belief that virtue could be measured in carbon credits and that social good could be indexed on a balance sheet. It gave hedge funds the illusion of righteousness and central bankers the language of salvation. And Carney, standing at the intersection of global capital and global governance, was its high priest.

But as Brookfield's acquisitions spread—into housing, energy, and public infrastructure—a glaring conflict of interest emerged, especially in Canada.

Brookfield began buying up sustainable housing developments, infrastructure assets, and even pre-manufactured home companies in Europe—just as Carney advised governments, including Canada's, on solving the housing crisis with new models of "net-zero" construction. He was shaping policy while standing to profit from its outcomes.

This wasn't mere coincidence. It was a systemic problem: the revolving door between public policy and private profit had become a conveyor belt. And Canada, always desperate for global approval, seemed unwilling to question it.

Carney, as always, deflected criticism by invoking noble aims—saving the planet, modernizing capitalism, promoting inclusive finance. But behind the press releases and glossy ESG brochures, a new consolidation of power was taking place. The power to allocate capital, define morality, and set the boundaries of permissible commerce had moved not to parliaments—but to investment committees and "transition funds."

With Carney at the center.

"Green" had become the new gold—and Carney, its alchemist.

He wasn't elected, but he was shaping climate strategy for entire nations.

He wasn't regulated, but he was helping to write the regulations that defined ESG compliance.

He wasn't running for office—yet—but he was increasingly being positioned as the man who could save capitalism from itself.

In truth, Carney hadn't saved anything.

He had merely ensured that the next phase of elite control would be more palatable to the public—not by changing the game, but by changing its language.

And Brookfield? They didn't mind.

After all, there's no better business model than saving the world... as long as you own it.

Chair of ESG and Transition Investing

When Mark Carney was appointed Chair of ESG and Transition Investing at Brookfield Asset Management, the role was marketed as a natural progression of his public service. In reality, it was the next phase of a carefully curated convergence between global policy, private capital, and unelected power.

This wasn't a ceremonial chairmanship. Carney was handed the reins of a portfolio designed not just to respond to global climate policy—but to shape it.

Brookfield's transition strategy, under Carney's leadership, involved massive investments in renewable energy, carbon markets, and net-zero infrastructure projects. On paper, it looked like benevolence with a Bloomberg terminal. In practice, it was elite monopoly disguised as virtue.

As Chair of ESG and Transition Investing, Carney had two primary levers of influence:

Control of narrative – He championed the language of climate justice and net-zero transitions, positioning Brookfield as a model of responsible capitalism.

Control of capital – He directed billions of dollars into asset classes that benefited from the very regulations and disclosures he helped design and promote as a UN Special Envoy and head of the TCFD.

This is not speculation. It is systemic design.

Carney's role as Chair effectively blended the world of public advocacy with private gain, creating a situation where Brookfield could acquire assets ahead of policy shifts that Carney himself was lobbying for. It was the ultimate insider advantage, sanctioned by media applause and cloaked in climate-conscious branding.

It wasn't enough to push ESG as a metric—Carney sought to institutionalize it. That meant new reporting frameworks, disclosure requirements, and scoring mechanisms, all of which tilted investment toward Brookfield's portfolio. The result? A redefinition of what it meant to be "sustainable"—one increasingly aligned with Carney's playbook.

Under his chairmanship, ESG morphed from an aspirational buzzword into a regulatory weapon—used to corral capital, influence national infrastructure spending, and consolidate control over the very definition of "transition."

By leading Brookfield's ESG arm, Carney wasn't just building a green portfolio. He was engineering the financial and moral architecture of the next global economy.

One where only those playing by the elite's "green rules" get funded.

One where the line between climate policy and capital allocation is so thin it barely exists.

And one where, conveniently, those who write the rules also own the assets.

## The Multi-Billion-Dollar Intersection of Climate and Capital

Mark Carney's career has been about many things—central banking, diplomacy, media-savvy statesmanship—but its defining hallmark is his uncanny ability to position himself at the most lucrative intersections of power. Nowhere is this more evident than in the emerging nexus where climate policy meets global finance: a space that has gone from obscure think tank theory to multi-trillion-dollar opportunity in under a decade.

Climate change was once framed as a moral crisis. Under Carney's stewardship, it has become a monetizable asset class.

From his roles at the United Nations, the Bank of England, and Brookfield Asset Management, Carney has quietly spearheaded a movement to reshape the very fabric of the global financial system under the banner of climate action. The goal? Redirect the flows of capital away from "brown" assets (like oil and gas) and into "green" assets (like renewables, carbon credits, and infrastructure labeled as sustainable). In doing so, an entirely new financial order is being born—one based not on market competition or democratic debate, but on elite certifications of moral virtue.

This isn't environmentalism. It's financial technocracy with a conscience-shaped mask.

In his role with the Task Force on Climate-related Financial Disclosures (TCFD) and as co-founder of the Glasgow Financial Alliance for Net Zero (GFANZ), Carney helped bring over $130 trillion in managed assets into alignment with ESG and net-zero targets. These weren't small environmental NGOs. These were pension funds, sovereign wealth funds, and the largest asset managers on Earth—BlackRock, State Street, HSBC, JPMorgan.

And yet, these funds didn't "go green" out of goodwill. They did so because the frameworks Carney helped develop began to dictate where and how investment could flow. Once codified into financial regulation and risk assessments, these frameworks effectively rewired the plumbing of the system. ESG didn't remain a choice—it became a compliance mandate.

That mandate now affects:

What companies are allowed to borrow

What projects receive public infrastructure funding

What firms qualify for insurance or subsidies

What investment vehicles are deemed acceptable for pension funds

The prize for those who play by the rules is massive—access to guaranteed capital at the expense of competitors. The penalty for those who don't? Financial suffocation.

And here's the rub: Carney sits in both chairs.

He's the regulator and the investor. The architect of the scoring system and the director of the fund. He advises governments and then invests through Brookfield in the assets those governments are forced to subsidize, greenlight, or privilege. It is the financialization of planetary stewardship, and the stakes are enormous—not only for capital, but for democratic control.

Once climate becomes capital, the climate conversation becomes captured by those who already control capital. It's not about saving the planet—it's about who gets to profit from managing the panic.

This intersection—where policy meets portfolio, where virtue becomes valuation—isn't a side hustle for Carney. It's his main act. He has transformed the climate crisis into a global restructuring opportunity, and in doing so, ensured that those already at the top of the pyramid remain there—but now with green halos.

The message is subtle but clear:

If you want to be part of the future, you'll need to buy your virtue—and Carney has just the fund to sell it to you.

# Chapter 6: The UN Climate Czar

In 2019, Mark Carney took the next step in consolidating his public image—not as a central banker or financier, but as a planetary savior. His appointment as UN Special Envoy on Climate Action and Finance by Secretary-General António Guterres was less a surprise than it was a confirmation: Carney was no longer merely a figure in national or corporate governance—he was now being positioned as one of the most influential voices in the global restructuring of civilization under the pretext of planetary survival.

It was a seamless move.

By this point, Carney had already helped engineer the rise of ESG (Environmental, Social, and Governance metrics) through his work at the Bank of England, the Financial Stability Board, and his partnership with entities like the World Economic Forum. Now, with the full weight of the United Nations behind him, he was poised to build the political and financial architecture that would cement climate finance as the backbone of global policy.

This was not climate action in the grassroots sense. It was a top-down corporate salvation narrative, with Carney as its spokesperson and high priest.

A Savior with a Rolodex

Carney's value to the UN was not in his environmental passion—it was in his Rolodex. He brought access to the world's most powerful financial institutions, from BlackRock to Brookfield, from Goldman Sachs to central banks across the G7. Under his leadership, the Glasgow

Financial Alliance for Net Zero (GFANZ) quickly amassed over $130 trillion in committed assets, uniting some 450 firms to accelerate the so-called "transition economy."

This wasn't diplomacy. It was financial consolidation on a planetary scale, framed in the moral language of salvation.

In press releases and conference halls, Carney framed the fight against climate change as a matter of economic realism. But behind the veil, what was being built was a new compliance regime—one in which your access to capital, trade, and legitimacy would be filtered through climate scoring systems that Carney and his associates helped define. These scoring systems were anything but democratic.

And yet, the narrative was irresistible: Only through unified action from governments, corporations, and financial giants can we avoid global catastrophe. In this framework, public dissent could be painted as denial, and central planning could be sold as collective salvation.

The Shadow of Sovereignty

What Carney represented was a profound shift in global governance. His role at the UN was a textbook example of how unelected, unaccountable actors can use supranational platforms to shape economic and political outcomes across the globe. National sovereignty, democratic debate, and regional diversity were seen as inconvenient obstacles to the uniformity required for "climate resilience."

But resilience, as Carney defined it, was less about ecological balance and more about capital liquidity in the face of systemic risk. His job wasn't to save the planet—it was to build an investment environment that could profit from its transformation. Through his envoy role, Carney helped translate the apocalypse into an asset class.

Under his watch, the UN climate agenda became a tool for financial alignment, not popular will. Every declaration, every net-zero summit, every green finance mandate—each one carried the subtle fingerprints of Carney's doctrine:

**Control the rules. Control the funding. Control the future.**

One Man, Many Hats

It is crucial to understand that Carney's UN appointment did not conflict with his other roles—it enhanced them. He remained Vice Chair at Brookfield, a member of the World Economic Forum's board of trustees, and a behind-the-scenes player in Canadian Liberal Party strategy. Each position reinforced the others, allowing him to leverage public trust to advance private capital, and vice versa.

This unprecedented concentration of influence under the veneer of virtue is what makes Carney so dangerous to democratic accountability. As UN envoy, he can recommend policies. As an asset manager, he can fund the winners. As a central banker, he can pressure the laggards. As a public intellectual, he can sanctify the entire apparatus.

Mark Carney isn't saving the planet.
He's restructuring it—from the boardroom down.

And for those who think this is just another technocratic shuffle, consider this: once environmental policy becomes a function of debt rating and investment scoring, the future belongs not to those who adapt, but to those who own the levers of transition.

Carney built those levers—and now he tells the world how to pull them.

Turning Environmental Crisis into Economic Opportunity

While the world panics over rising sea levels and wildfires, Mark Carney and his elite counterparts have been quietly setting up the ultimate extraction economy—not from the Earth itself, but from the crisis surrounding it. At the core of this new regime are instruments like carbon credits and green bonds: financial tools that, in theory, help reduce emissions—but in practice, concentrate power, wealth, and control.

Let's start with carbon credits.

In Carney's new economy, carbon is no longer simply a pollutant—it is a currency. The idea is deceptively simple: a company that emits less than its allotted share of greenhouse gases can sell the unused portion of its emissions allowance to another company that exceeds its limit. This creates a market for pollution—a legalized indulgence system where the worst offenders don't have to reform, they just have to pay.

Enter Carney's allies in asset management and institutional finance.

Rather than treating carbon credits as a temporary stopgap or regulatory nudge, these groups have turned the system into a complex web of derivatives, portfolios, and speculations—a new frontier for profit. Major polluters purchase cheap credits from developing nations, where so-called "offset projects" often lack oversight, transparency, or permanence. Forests are pledged and then logged. Communities are displaced in the name of conservation. The math doesn't matter. The illusion of compliance does.

And who oversees this shell game?

Organizations tied to the very architects of the system.

**The Rise of Green Bonds**

While carbon credits allow companies to buy moral legitimacy, green bonds let governments and corporations borrow it.

A green bond is essentially a regular bond with a green label slapped on it. It's supposed to fund projects that combat climate change or promote sustainability. In practice, however, green bonds have little accountability, vague terms, and open doors to greenwashing on a global scale. A freeway expansion with bike lanes? Green bond eligible. A solar array that displaces poor farmers? Green stamp it. A lithium mine for electric cars? That's ESG gold.

Mark Carney has been one of the most vocal champions of green finance. His message is always the same: if the market won't act fast enough, we need to redirect capital by any means necessary. He speaks not as a regulator, but as a missionary for financial salvation, using lan guage that blends moral urgency with technocratic manipulation.

This is not the economy fixing the planet.

This is the planet being mortgaged to save the economy.

The New Gatekeepers of Capital

In this green financial utopia, Carney and his peers present themselves as benevolent stewards, shepherding the global economy toward a net-zero future. But behind the slogans, a very different reality emerges: a two-tiered system where access to funding, legitimacy, and survival is gated behind compliance with opaque ESG criteria.

Who defines those criteria?

The same financial elites that stand to benefit.

Companies are now scored not on their real contributions to sustainability, but on their ability to check boxes, manipulate metrics, and appease consulting firms that sell ESG verification as a product. This makes ESG less a moral compass than a profit algorithm. The better your ESG score, the better your access to capital. For everyone else? Closed doors and virtue lectures.

This is the new cartel:

Climate-certified monopolists who lock out competitors, crush dissent, and rebrand tyranny as stewardship.

The Crisis-to-Cash Pipeline

For Carney and his network, crisis is not just opportunity—it's infrastructure. Climate panic provides the perfect justification to centralize control, issue trillions in public and private debt, and build permanent systems of compliance in every sector of life.

Carbon credits, green bonds, ESG scores—they all share a hidden logic: convert planetary guilt into speculative assets, then sell those assets to the public as progress.

This is the future:

A world where billionaires own carbon while the rest of us rent air.

And the man at the center of it—the diplomat, the investor, the regulator, the visionary—is Mark Carney, architect of a climate regime that profits from crisis while pretending to prevent it.

He doesn't just green the economy.

He gold-plates the scam.

One of the least scrutinized but most consequential aspects of Mark Carney's career is his role in accelerating the quiet privatization of global climate governance. While the media portrays his trajectory as a seamless integration of public service and enlightened capitalism, what actually emerges is a blueprint for how unelected elites can dominate the most urgent issue of our time—climate change—by wrapping old financial power structures in the green veneer of ESG rhetoric and carbon accounting.

Carney's appointment as the UN Special Envoy for Climate Action and Finance was not the beginning of this trajectory—it was its culmination. From that platform, he set in motion a new phase of globalization, not grounded in democratic consensus or ecological stewardship, but in financial instruments, shadow banking, and top-down target setting. His main initiative, the Glasgow Financial Alliance for Net Zero (GFANZ), represents the apex of this new climate order: a consortium of banks, investment funds, and insurance firms, collectively pledging trillions toward a net-zero transition. It sounds noble until one realizes who actually sets the rules.

There was no popular vote for GFANZ. No public oversight body was formed to vet its leadership or direction. Yet Carney and his network now influence where capital flows, which technologies receive investment, and what standards count as "green." The very language of sustainability has been captured—not by activists or sovereign governments—but by market-makers and private equity managers. Instead of public law, we get private frameworks. Instead of transparency, we get branded reports and asset-weighted lobbying. And always, at the center of it all, Carney, exuding quiet certainty, technocratic charm, and the full confidence of Davos.

What makes this more dangerous than older forms of corporate overreach is its invisibility. Traditional privatization involves selling off public goods—rail lines, power grids, health systems. But climate governance is not owned in the same way. It's a shared planetary concern, a commons. And Carney has helped redraw its boundaries, shifting influence from public mandates to financial consensus. Through carbon markets, sustainability-linked bonds, and institutional investor panels, he and his allies have effectively built a parallel government—one that cannot be unelected, and one that does not have to answer to the people most affected by the decisions it makes.

This is not just technocracy—it is capture. Environmental capture. Semantic capture. Policy capture. By the time governments react, if they ever do, it may already be too late to reclaim control. Carney isn't saving the world. He's consolidating it. One financial agreement at a time.

# Chapter 7: The King's Privy Council

The King's Privy Council for Canada is one of the most obscure but powerful instruments of government in the country—hidden in plain sight. It is a formal body of advisors to the Crown, originally modeled on its British counterpart, and though most Canadians have never heard of it, this unelected group continues to wield immense influence behind the scenes. On paper, its function is ceremonial, a vestige of monarchy meant to advise the sovereign. In practice, it is a constitutional loophole that consolidates executive power in a way that bypasses parliamentary accountability and shields insiders from public scrutiny.

The Privy Council's membership includes past and present ministers, Supreme Court justices, Governors General, and elite insiders like Mark Carney—who, despite holding no elected office, was appointed to the council in 2022. This raises the obvious question: why would a former central banker, with no direct mandate from the people, be formally empowered to advise the Crown? The answer lies in how Canada has quietly allowed the Crown's legal architecture to persist long after its political relevance should have expired. The Privy Council exists at the interface of legacy and legal fiction, a shadow structure of continuity that enables power without exposure.

When Carney was sworn into the Privy Council, it wasn't just a symbolic nod to his status—it was a calculated elevation. It guaranteed him access. It tied him directly to the state without tethering him to public accountability. It gave him the formal gravitas of a statesman without requiring the vulnerability of an election. And it signals that the Canadian state sees no contradiction in embedding elite globalist bankers inside its most protected constitutional mechanisms.

This is the kind of institutional arrangement that polite democracies like Canada use to obscure real power. The Privy Council, alongside the Governor General and other Crown instruments, allows the government to operate in a mode that feels democratic while retaining the discretionary levers of autocracy. Orders-in-Council—binding legal decisions issued through the Privy Council—can implement sweeping changes without parliamentary debate. And when the public reacts, the response is often procedural: "This is how it's always been."

But "how it's always been" is not a justification. It is a deflection. Carney's placement within this institution is not accidental—it's strategic. It situates him above politics and beneath public awareness, at the intersection of global finance and national sovereignty. From this perch, he can influence policy direction, climate finance, banking regulation, and intergovernmental coordination—all without ever subjecting himself to the risks that come with democratic representation.

The King's Privy Council is, in essence, an anachronism weaponized for modern governance. It is monarchy's last smokescreen, and Carney, ever the strategist, has made it part of his path to power. Canadians should be asking: when influence hides behind ceremony, when the levers of state are handed to private financiers, and when ancient institutions become modern tools of elite consolidation—are we still living in a democracy, or just a curated illusion of one?

Mark Carney's appointment to the King's Privy Council in 2022 was not accompanied by a press conference, media blitz, or even the usual self-congratulatory soundbites from Ottawa. It happened silently—almost surgically—through a bland Order-in-Council buried on a government website. No announcement, no explanation, and most tellingly, no questions from a media class either asleep at the wheel or complicit in its silence.

This lack of coverage wasn't an oversight. It was a tactic. Carney's ascent into the highest circles of government power, despite holding no elected office and answering to no democratic process, was handled like a matter of routine. But there is nothing routine about placing a former central banker, a Wall Street veteran, and globalist ideologue into the King's inner circle of Crown advisors. It represents a fundamental breach of the democratic spirit, if not its hollowed-out structure.

Appointments to the Privy Council are for life. They grant not just symbolic status but privileged access—access to confidential briefings, decision-making bodies, and an insider's influence over government machinery. This makes Carney, on paper, a formal advisor to the Crown—the same legal foundation that underpins the power of the prime minister and the cabinet. And yet, no Canadian voted for him. He stood for no office. He subjected none of his ideas—whether on ESG, digital currency, or climate capitalism—to debate. Instead, he was elevated silently, like a bishop in a smoke-filled conclave.

The implications are stark. This appointment effectively grants Carney a state-sanctioned platform to shape national policy from the shadows. And it does so while bypassing the transparency and accountability that ought to govern public life. The man whose career has been defined by backroom financial deals, Davos panels, and closed-door think tanks is now constitutionally embedded in the Canadian power structure, without a single headline or public reckoning.

Even more troubling is the timing. His appointment occurred during a period of active political positioning—amid rumors of a Liberal leadership bid, UN roles, and growing entanglement with private equity juggernauts like Brookfield. The optics are clear: Carney is being handed the keys to the kingdom before the public even knows there's a succession plan. This is not just undemocratic—it's post-democratic. It assumes the public is no longer part of the process, only part of the scenery.

In any functioning democracy, such an appointment would have sparked debate. But in Canada, it passed like a whisper through Parliament Hill. No opposition uproar. No media interrogation. Just a quiet nod from the technocratic elite that one of their own had been positioned exactly where he belongs—above scrutiny, beneath ceremony, and behind the green curtain of power.

The silent appointment of Mark Carney should be seen for what it is: a warning. It signals that Canada's institutional machinery is no longer even pretending to be accountable. That decisions of enormous consequence—like who shapes policy and advises the Crown—are no longer made in public. They are made in private. In silence. And always in service of the same narrow class of global managers who never stop reminding us that they know best.

Mark Carney's career is not just a case study in upward mobility—it's a living indictment of how modern democracies have been slowly gutted in favor of elite governance. While the average citizen is conditioned to believe that elections, debates, and public accountability still matter, figures like Carney quietly ascend through the backchannels of power, answering to no constituency but always appearing at the center of major decisions.

Democracy, in its ideal form, implies that political power is derived from the people. But Carney's rise shows us how power increasingly comes from somewhere else—namely, financial institutions, supranational organizations, and unaccountable corporate interests. He did not build a political platform. He was not vetted by voters. He was installed—by global banking firms, central banks, UN councils, and private investment boards—all acting as scaffolding for an international class of technocrats who govern with the appearance of objectivity and the immunity of royalty.

In Carney's world, governance doesn't flow from citizen consent. It flows from corporate balance sheets, ESG frameworks, and climate compliance metrics. It's rule by data, not by dialogue—where the language of financial optimization replaces political philosophy. In this model, technocracy masquerades as democracy, and Carney is its polished frontman.

The real brilliance of this system lies in its ability to sell the public on its own marginalization. The population is told that Carney's type of governance is apolitical, rational, even benevolent. That men in suits with credentials from Oxford and board positions at Brookfield know better than millions of messy, emotional voters. But this is not post-partisanship—it is post-democracy. A system where the major decisions about finance, climate, energy, and infrastructure are made in green rooms and summits, not in town halls or parliaments.

Carney exemplifies this shift. He doesn't seek power through the ballot box; he assumes it by default, through appointments, panels, and advisory roles. He sidesteps debate because his legitimacy isn't earned from the public—it's conferred by the elite. This isn't conspiracy—it's structure. It's how modern governance now works: quiet, opaque, and completely insulated from democratic will.

And the real danger is that most people don't even notice. Because the mechanisms of influence have changed. Because public consent has been replaced with stakeholder input. Because democracy has been bypassed—elegantly, efficiently, and with barely a whisper.

# Chapter 8: The Trudeau Connection

Mark Carney's political influence in Canada cannot be fully understood without unpacking his close and calculated alignment with Justin Trudeau. What might appear on the surface as a mere friendship between two Ivy-educated, urbane progressives is in fact one of the most consequential alliances in the quiet remodeling of Canada into a technocratic outpost of global governance.

Trudeau, the son of political royalty and the poster boy of global liberalism, needed credibility. Not just charisma, but intellectual weight—someone who could sell the most radical shifts in policy under the guise of economic stability and moral responsibility. Enter Carney: a man who oozes elite legitimacy, with credentials that read like a globalist résumé—Goldman Sachs, the Bank of Canada, the Bank of England, the United Nations, and Brookfield. He was a dream come true for a Prime Minister looking to reframe government overreach as enlightened stewardship.

The timing was no coincidence. As Trudeau pushed Canada further into ESG mandates, net-zero pledges, pandemic-era authoritarianism, and massive fiscal spending, Carney appeared in the wings, always ready with a quote, a policy paper, or a closed-door briefing. He was Canada's shadow economist, the unelected intellectual architect of much of the federal agenda—particularly around climate finance, energy transition, and "stakeholder capitalism."

They share more than just talking points. Trudeau and Carney are united by worldview—a deep belief in managerialism, global institutions, and the idea that the public must be guided, not persuaded. In this relationship, Carney is the mind, and Trudeau the mouthpiece. It is a partnership of presentation and policy, of charm and charts.

When speculation began swirling about Carney's possible entry into formal politics, it wasn't a question of if he'd join Trudeau's team—it was a matter of optics and timing. Would he come in through the front door, or would he continue steering policy through the back halls of the Privy Council, the Bank of Canada, and Davos?

The answer so far has been the latter. Because why risk election when you already run the ship? With Trudeau as the face of "sunny ways," Carney remains the unaccountable force behind the curtain, quietly shaping Canada's monetary policy, climate commitments, and economic narrative through speeches, strategic placements, and a revolving door of influence.

Their relationship isn't just about mutual respect—it's about shared intent. Both men believe in a post-national, post-democratic Canada governed by data, modeling, and global consensus—not by the consent of its people. Carney didn't need to win over voters. He won over Trudeau—and that, in today's Ottawa, is more than enough.

Mark Carney and Justin Trudeau are not merely political allies by convenience—they are ideological twins, reflecting a shared vision of a post-democratic, technocratic Canada ruled by elite consensus rather than electoral accountability. Their policies echo each other not by accident, but by design. What Trudeau signs into law, Carney has often spoken, written, or signaled in advance through speeches at Davos, policy papers, or financial forums. The synchronization is uncanny—and deliberate.

Take climate policy. Trudeau's carbon pricing, aggressive net-zero targets, and push to phase out traditional energy sources follow the script Carney has laid out for years. Carney's speeches as UN Climate Envoy, and his work at Brookfield, didn't just influence Canada's direction—they mirror it. Their shared obsession with ESG metrics, climate bonds, and "green" financial instruments reflect a core belief: that public good can be managed like a portfolio, and the future of Canada should be decided in boardrooms, not town halls.

Or consider central banking and fiscal policy. Trudeau's massive pandemic-era spending, inflation-ignoring stimulus, and willingness to blur the lines between central bank independence and political necessity all track with Carney's long-standing belief that monetary and fiscal policy must be merged in the face of crisis—whether that crisis is a virus, a climate model, or a social equity metric. Both men view the economy less as a free-market organism and more as a technocratic engine to be steered toward global goals.

Even immigration, digital identity, and censorship policies reveal the sync. Carney has been vocally pro-mass immigration—not as a compassionate stance, but as a labor-market tool. Trudeau's border policies reflect this utilitarianism masked in humanitarian rhetoric. Carney has also promoted the role of digital currencies and digital IDs as tools for managing climate behavior and social compliance—precisely the terrain Trudeau has been slowly walking Canadians into under the guise of innovation and safety.

Most revealing is their shared tone. Both speak in vague, lofty moralism while executing deeply centralized, top-down governance strategies. They rely on "stakeholders," "equity," and "resilience" as euphemisms for control, consolidation, and managed decline. The public doesn't get clarity—it gets narratives. And those narratives are cooked in the same ideological kitchen.

Ultimately, Carney and Trudeau represent the same class of global managerialism. Whether speaking as a banker or a politician, their core belief is the same: that ordinary Canadians cannot be trusted with the future of their country. That task, they believe, belongs to the right people—with the right credentials—making the right decisions behind closed doors. Together, they have redefined governance not as representation, but as stewardship. And that is the most dangerous alignment of all.

The idea of Mark Carney returning to Canada not as a banker, but as Prime Minister, is no longer a fringe theory—it is a probability being quietly groomed into inevitability. He is the global elite's chosen man, the silver bullet of technocratic governance, and the insurance policy of Canada's liberal establishment. His potential ascent to the highest office is not based on democratic groundswell or popular support—it is being orchestrated by the same apparatus that ensures continuity of agenda, not accountability to the people.

Carney doesn't need to campaign in the traditional sense. He's already built his resume in the smoke-filled rooms of Davos and the gated boardrooms of Brookfield. As Governor of both the Bank of Canada and the Bank of England, he's curated an image of financial stability while quietly pushing the ideological transformation of monetary policy into a vehicle for social engineering. His appointment as UN Climate Czar was a crowning achievement for the global managerial class—a soft coronation that announced his availability to rule not just markets, but nations.

What should concern Canadians isn't just that Carney may run—it's that there will be no meaningful choice left when he does. His political positioning, much like Trudeau's, relies on virtue-signaling, climate orthodoxy, and the language of inclusion—all while centralizing power into institutions the public doesn't elect and cannot challenge. He will speak of sustainability while handing infrastructure to foreign firms. He will invoke equity while setting ESG compliance as the new test for loans, business licenses, and employment access. And like Trudeau, he will outsource national sovereignty to global accords and multilateral pacts that bypass Parliament entirely.

But Carney isn't just another politician—he is a representative of the post-political. He does not need a constituency. His power is in networks, in capital, in systems. His return is the manifestation of everything technocracy desires: rule by unelected, unaccountable experts who speak in metrics, manage in algorithms, and hide behind "the science."

The Liberal Party knows it cannot win the next election on Trudeau's name alone. That brand is fading, scorched by scandal, division, and fatigue. Carney is their pivot. He is the fresh face with the same agenda—the next mask of managerialism. His globalism will be marketed as pragmatism. His aloofness reframed as professionalism. His disinterest in Canadian identity will be sold as cosmopolitan sophistication.

But beneath that polished exterior lies a cold calculus: a Canada steered not by its citizens, but by its creditors; not by its culture, but by its compliance score; not by its dreams, but by its ESG metrics.

Mark Carney doesn't just want to govern—he wants to complete the transformation of governance itself. His return must be understood not as a political candidacy, but as a consolidation of corporate, global, and institutional power into the office of the Prime Minister.

It won't be an election. It will be a coronation. Unless Canadians wake up first.

# Chapter 9: The WEF Playbook

Mark Carney's relationship with the World Economic Forum (WEF) and its founder Klaus Schwab is not peripheral—it is central to understanding his role in shaping the emerging global architecture of control. The WEF's now-notorious agenda of the "Great Reset" is not just a slogan—it is a comprehensive blueprint for replacing free-market democracies with "stakeholder capitalism," a euphemism for corporate and bureaucratic hegemony. At the heart of that model is Mark Carney.

Carney and Schwab are ideological twins—both believe that the era of national sovereignty, traditional democracy, and private enterprise is obsolete. In its place, they envision a world where unelected technocrats, multinational corporations, and transnational institutions collaborate to set global policy without interference from voters. It's not a conspiracy—it's printed in the white papers, spoken at Davos panels, and openly implemented in policy.

Carney's speeches at the WEF are not passive endorsements. He is a principal architect of its economic agenda. He has called for a "fundamental reshaping of finance," where private capital is harnessed not for profit, but for "climate justice," "social equity," and other ESG-aligned priorities. But in practice, this means rerouting capital toward politically favored industries, censoring credit from politically disfavored ones, and embedding ideological criteria into the very DNA of the economy.

Through the WEF, Carney has advanced the idea of the "Stakeholder Corporation," a Trojan horse concept that displaces the shareholder (owner and investor) model with a system where corporations answer instead to amorphous "stakeholders" like NGOs, international bureaucracies, or activist boards. In reality, this means no accountability to the customer or investor, and complete alignment with the goals of supranational agendas—such as net-zero targets, DEI metrics, or digital identification systems.

The Stakeholder State is not built in legislatures. It is built through frameworks, banking regulations, trade rules, procurement policies, and social scoring systems. Carney has been a key player in embedding ESG into the financial system, ensuring that only those who conform to the ideological line can access loans, funding, and markets. It is a soft form of authoritarianism, hidden beneath the language of sustainability and responsibility.

Schwab may have written the playbook, but Carney is executing it in real time. From Brookfield to the UN, from the Bank of England to his shadow role in Canadian politics, Carney is not just implementing policy—he is restructuring the system itself.

The ultimate vision? A world where power no longer flows from the citizen to the government, but from the unelected institutional elite to the compliant citizen. Where governance is no longer accountable to voters, but to data. Where metrics replace morals, and social engineering is a balance sheet operation.

This is the stakeholder future Mark Carney is building—a world where the rules are written by those who don't have to follow them, and enforced on those who never got to vote.

Stakeholder capitalism and sovereign democracy are not complementary ideas—they are rival systems competing for control of society's future. One roots power in the ballot box, the other in the boardroom. One recognizes the individual as the sovereign unit of political agency; the other sees the individual as a managed asset within a global ledger of compliance, equity, and sustainability.

Mark Carney, more than perhaps any other public figure, embodies the shift from democracy to stakeholder rule. His vision of capitalism is no longer about serving consumers or delivering returns to investors. Instead, it is about aligning capital with political and social goals set not by citizens, but by elite institutions and ideological frameworks—many of which are unelected, unaccountable, and largely invisible to the average person.

In sovereign democracy, accountability flows upward from the individual to the institutions. You elect representatives. They pass laws. You have a say, however limited, in shaping the rules that govern your life.

Stakeholder capitalism inverts this. It replaces elected accountability with ESG metrics, diversity audits, climate pledges, and social equity mandates determined by supranational bodies, international financial institutions, and corporate "values committees." Voters do not choose these rules. They do not debate them. They inherit them, pre-packaged and non-negotiable.

Under stakeholder capitalism, companies are not expected to serve their owners or customers. They are expected to serve "stakeholders"—a term so vague it can be filled with whatever ideological agenda the managerial class currently embraces. Today, that means climate targets, racial equity indexes, and social credit systems disguised as corporate policy.

Carney defends this as responsible leadership. In truth, it is a backdoor to soft totalitarianism. It replaces the slow, messy, accountable process of democracy with an efficient, opaque process of enforced consensus. The new metrics become law without legislation. Dissent becomes disinvestment. Political difference becomes economic exclusion.

The danger is not hypothetical—it is already unfolding. Banks deny service based on ideology. Investment firms with trillions under management redirect global capital based on ESG scores. Whole sectors are being restructured not by competition, but by ideological compliance. All while the democratic voter becomes increasingly irrelevant to the economic system they supposedly own.

Stakeholder capitalism is not capitalism at all. It is a planned economy run by planners you can't name, for goals you didn't choose. It doesn't fix the failures of capitalism—it simply adds a layer of coercion disguised as morality.

The future of freedom depends on exposing this model for what it is: an elite-driven replacement for self-government. One where climate panels replace parliaments, and financial nudging replaces constitutional rights. The question is not whether Carney's system is more efficient. The question is whether it's ours to reject.

If democracy means anything, it must mean the right to say no—to ESG, to unelected power, to technocratic utopianism wrapped in the language of justice. Sovereign democracy is not perfect. But it is ours. Stakeholder capitalism, by contrast, was never up for a vote.

Redefining capitalism without a vote is the silent revolution of our age.

It doesn't come through coups or constitutions, but through boardrooms, central banks, and international summits—places where policies are written not by elected representatives but by economists, financiers, and bureaucrats who answer to no electorate.

Mark Carney stands at the helm of this shift. Through roles at the Bank of Canada, Bank of England, Brookfield, and the United Nations, he has become one of the chief architects of a new global consensus—one in which capitalism is no longer judged by free enterprise or voluntary exchange, but by how well it serves political goals cloaked in morality: net zero, equity, sustainability, inclusion. Buzzwords that sound virtuous but conceal something far more radical—a restructuring of the economic order from the top down.

Under this redefinition, profit is no longer the measure of success. Compliance is. Companies must now align not only with markets but with metrics—ESG scores, diversity audits, climate targets—all set by institutions outside the democratic process. It is capitalism without capitalists, markets without consent, private enterprise managed by public ideology.

And it is happening without a vote.

Not one Canadian voted for the carbon offset market. Not one Briton elected Carney to reengineer the global economy. No referendum was held on whether BlackRock, Brookfield, and the World Economic Forum should become the new priests of progress.

The language has shifted, too. No longer do we speak of citizens and entrepreneurs. Now we have "stakeholders." But who decides who the stakeholders are? Who decides what values they must uphold? Who enforces the mandate when the people refuse to comply?

The answer is: people like Carney.

Behind the polished speeches about "building a better capitalism" lies the erasure of political choice. You can't vote ESG out. You can't recall your UN Special Envoy. You can't fire your central banker. The most powerful forces shaping your economic life are now beyond your reach.

This is not evolution. It is theft. Not of wealth, but of agency.

Real capitalism is rooted in consent and competition. What we are witnessing is a technocratic redesign—a capitalism engineered by elites who believe they know better than the people, and who will quietly impose their blueprint whether the people agree or not.

This is not a bug in the system. It is the system.

Redefining capitalism without a vote is the final betrayal of liberal democracy. Because once economic freedom is redefined from above, political freedom becomes a formality. The ballot box becomes symbolic. The economy becomes a behavioral compliance machine.

The only question that remains is: will we notice before it's too late?

# Chapter 10: The Digital Dollar & Surveillance

Mark Carney has always spoken the language of modernization. But in the realm of money, that language is now being used to erase one of the last remaining forms of individual autonomy—cash. His championing of Central Bank Digital Currencies (CBDCs) is framed as innovation, inclusion, and efficiency. In reality, it is the gateway to a financial surveillance grid with no precedent in history.

Carney's public advocacy for a digital currency began as early as his tenure at the Bank of England. He suggested that in a world where "Amazon and Facebook are creating private monies," central banks must act or lose control. The message was clear: the state must remain the sole master of money, even if it means digitizing every transaction, every account, every citizen's financial behavior.

At Brookfield and through his roles with the UN and WEF, Carney's voice has grown louder—not only promoting digital currencies but also linking them directly with ESG compliance, carbon credit tracking, and social governance metrics. This is not a libertarian crypto-utopia. This is programmable money, designed from the top down. Money with strings.

Imagine a future where your spending habits are tied to your carbon footprint. Where your bank account can be frozen for misinformation or political protest. Where social credit is enforced not with police, but by the denial of access to basic economic tools. Under a CBDC regime, this isn't science fiction—it's infrastructure.

Carney and his peers portray this transformation as "democratizing finance." In truth, it centralizes power in the hands of unelected bureaucrats and private partners. The architecture of surveillance—already dominant in Big Tech—is being fused with the tools of monetary control. Every purchase, every donation, every moment of economic choice becomes legible to the state.

No longer is money a private medium of exchange. It becomes a ledger of behavior. Not just what you spend, but where, on what, and why. "Compliance" becomes the currency, and deviation from the approved values gets quietly punished through digital throttling.

The danger is not just economic—it's civilizational. Cash is freedom. Cash is friction. And in that friction, there is privacy, dissent, and the ability to operate outside the eye of centralized power. CBDCs eliminate that. They create a society where not only is everything tracked, but everything can be controlled—remotely, algorithmically, and without appeal.

Carney calls this the future of inclusive finance.

It is, instead, a new form of feudalism.

Feudal lords used to extract rent in land and loyalty. Now the new lords, dressed in green, extract data and obedience. Under the guise of convenience and climate, Carney's digital dollar is being sold to a distracted public. But when it arrives, it will not liberate. It will lock down.

The question is not whether CBDCs will be implemented. The real question is: once they are, will freedom ever be able to claw its way back into the system?

Carney's grand design doesn't end with the digitization of money—it deepens with its integration into the ESG (Environmental, Social, and Governance) scoring apparatus. The next frontier of financial control is not simply knowing what you spend—it's judging what you spend it on. And it is here, at this intersection of ideology and economics, that the true nature of "stakeholder capitalism" is revealed: a system that rewards obedience and penalizes dissent—not through laws, but through your bank account.

In speeches and white papers, Carney has repeatedly hinted at this convergence. A digital currency—especially one issued by central banks—allows for programmable controls. This means every transaction can be evaluated in real time for compliance with carbon goals, social behavior targets, or governance standards. The moment you tap your phone to pay, the system can assign a value—not just a price, but a score.

Buying local, organic produce? Your ESG score goes up. Supporting an independent media outlet flagged for "misinformation"? Expect a flag on your profile. Want to donate to a political party outside the approved consensus? That may affect your future loan eligibility. It's not a system of overt prohibition. It's one of quiet discouragement. Of nudges and penalties. Of soft tyranny.

Under Carney's framework, your financial identity becomes a mirror of your ideological alignment. Carbon footprint trackers, already trialed by major banks in Europe, are the tip of the spear. Imagine energy quotas, consumption limits, or "green discounts" tied to lifestyle compliance. All administered not by elected legislators—but by algorithms written in back rooms by technocrats, NGOs, and corporations.

This is a world where "climate action" becomes the cover story for total compliance. Where your money is no longer yours to use freely—but a token of access granted by how well you toe the line. And once spending habits are monitored, ranked, and scored, the social contract is redefined: not between the citizen and the state, but between the individual and an unelected system of global values.

Carney's genius lies not in invention, but in translation. He has taken the climate crisis—a real and urgent issue—and transformed it into a justification for economic obedience. He speaks in the tones of moderation and consensus, but the infrastructure he promotes is radical: a financial regime where dissent is expensive, and conformity is rewarded.

This isn't capitalism. It's not socialism. It's a new techno-feudal order.

In it, ESG doesn't just shape investment—it shapes life. And every purchase becomes a confession.

The final phase of Carney's vision is the fusion of finance, behavior, and state control—a convergence so seamless it barely feels like control at all. It's dressed in the language of sustainability, equity, and digital convenience. But beneath the buzzwords lies a chilling proposition: that the state no longer needs to coerce when it can simply condition.

This new system won't arrive through jackboots or forced declarations. It will come through apps. Through nudges. Through the gentle redefinition of freedom into a permission slip.

You won't be told what to believe—you'll be priced into submission.

A digital currency, tied to a centralized ESG framework, turns your entire financial life into a dashboard of compliance. Carbon limits, health metrics, ideological preferences—each becomes a variable in your financial worthiness. Miss the mark, and you're not fined—you're excluded. Your mortgage rate goes up. Your access to credit tightens. Your transaction is denied. No judge. No jury. Just the cold decision of a machine optimized for "sustainable outcomes."

This is where Mark Carney matters most—not as a banker, but as a high priest of a new, post-democratic order. His speeches are the scripture of technocracy. His partnerships—from Brookfield to the UN to the WEF—are the institutional scaffolding. And his policies, slowly and quietly implemented, are not designed for nations—but for systems.

The digital dollar isn't a tool—it's a gateway. Once programmable money is deployed, the path is open for algorithmic governance. Behavior itself becomes currency. This is social credit, reframed for the West. Not declared—but implemented by proxy. Your rights, your resources, your reputation—managed by code.

In Carney's world, you'll still be able to vote. But increasingly, it won't matter. Because true power won't lie with parliaments—it will lie with platforms. With banks. With rating agencies and unelected councils. The state will enforce less, because the system will enforce more. Voluntary compliance becomes mandatory through engineered consequence.

This is not dystopia as warning. It is dystopia as rollout.

And unless it is named, challenged, and rejected—Carney's future will become our present.

# Chapter 11: Controlled Collapse

M ark Carney's career is often praised for calm stewardship during financial turbulence. But the deeper story—the one rarely told—is not of a man managing crises, but of a man managing the perception of crises, while quietly laying the groundwork for a controlled demolition of economic sovereignty.

Carney's fingerprints are all over the evolving financial playbook of managed inflation and interest rate manipulation. These are not reactive tools anymore—they're proactive levers used to reshape society. And behind the curtain, he and his technocratic peers have transformed central banking into a mechanism not of national stewardship, but of global coordination. What was once a tool to protect domestic economic stability is now being wielded to serve the interests of transnational capital, green industrial planning, and digital governance infrastructure.

Let's not forget: inflation is not a natural disaster. It is the product of policy. And during Carney's tenure—as head of both the Bank of Canada and the Bank of England—policies were repeatedly enacted that inflated asset bubbles, suppressed wage growth, and redistributed wealth upwards. The strategy was always the same: use artificially low interest rates and massive liquidity injections to "stimulate" the economy. But the stimulation was selective. It didn't lift main street—it levitated financial markets. It didn't empower workers—it enriched the asset-owning elite.

And when the inflationary consequences finally hit, central banks feigned surprise.

But Carney, with his usual rhetorical sleight of hand, would always frame inflation as a "transitory" side effect of global instability or market misalignment, while conveniently omitting the years of coordinated monetary overreach that set the stage. And when the hammer finally dropped—when rates were raised and credit conditions tightened—it was the working class who paid the price.

The result? A deliberately cultivated scarcity. Home ownership became a privilege of the investor class. Small businesses were squeezed to the brink. Essential goods became volatile luxuries. And basic services like energy and food—under the new banner of green transition—were bundled into a model of "managed deprivation." It's not failure. It's design.

This is the new financial reality: a game of engineered collapse. Not to destroy the system, but to consolidate control. To make the public dependent on a new class of technocratic overlords—green lenders, digital identity brokers, universal basic income distributors. Scarcity creates dependency. Dependency creates compliance.

Carney's playbook is not about free markets—it's about the simulation of markets under algorithmic control. His vision is a financial system that looks dynamic, but is in fact pre-programmed—one that uses crisis to accelerate consolidation and uses inflation as both a tool of debt servitude and an excuse for radical restructuring.

He didn't cause the global debt trap alone. But he knew exactly how to use it. He knew how to inflate assets, offload risk onto the public, and then walk away clean with a promotion, a fellowship, or a seat at the table of global governance. Every collapse became a stepping stone. Every rate hike, every liquidity freeze, every currency manipulation—a calculated step toward a more tightly controlled financial order.

What we're witnessing now isn't just incompetence. It's a strategy of attrition. A slow, systematic draining of middle-class autonomy under the guise of "fighting inflation," "saving the planet," or "stabilizing the economy."

It is not merely about money. It is about power. The power to starve a sector, bankrupt a class, or crash a currency—and to do so without a single vote being cast.

And Mark Carney remains at the center of that power.

**Who Benefits When Economies Are "Reset"?**

The short answer: not you.

When economists, central bankers, and World Economic Forum elites speak of an "economic reset," they are not referring to a reboot that restores prosperity to the average citizen. They are talking about re-architecting the global economy to suit the needs of a consolidated class—those who sit at the intersection of finance, technology, and governance.

Let's be blunt. Every "reset" we've witnessed—post-2008, post-COVID, post-inflation—has followed the same pattern: privatize the gains, socialize the losses, and centralize the control. It's a shell game. The destruction is public; the recovery is private.

Take the housing market. The crash wipes out millions of home-owners. Then BlackRock and Brookfield swoop in, backed by cheap money and state incentives, to buy up distressed assets. Overnight, the dream of homeownership becomes the reality of permanent tenancy. Who benefits? Not the family trying to buy their first home—but the institutional landlord who now controls your roof.

Or look at the currency devaluations and inflationary waves. They erode your purchasing power, shrink your savings, and saddle you with debt. But for hedge funds, sovereign wealth managers, and ESG-aligned megabanks, volatility is profit. These entities benefit from the chaos. They're hedged against collapse. They own the algorithms. They trade the future before you've even felt the present.

And when the reset calls for green energy or digital currency? It's not about freedom or sustainability—it's about control. The same elite that profited from oil now owns carbon markets. The same bankers that wrecked the global financial system are now rewriting the ESG metrics. The same governments that failed to protect your job now want programmable digital dollars that can expire or be restricted based on your "social compliance."

It's not just a reset. It's a reallocation—from you to them.

Every reset has beneficiaries. And those beneficiaries are always the ones who sit closest to the money spigot, the data servers, and the regulatory levers. They don't want to fix the economy—they want to own the new one. Preferably without the inconvenience of democracy, private property, or individual liberty getting in the way.

When Carney and his cohort use phrases like "Build Back Better" or "Just Transition," they are masking an uncomfortable truth: the old world is being dismantled, but the new one is not being built for you. It is being built around you. A world of subscriptions, not ownership. A world of allowances, not earnings. A world of enforced virtue, not voluntary morality.

So who benefits from the reset?

Those who caused the crash, wrote the bailout terms, redefined the narrative, and now want to control the rebuild.

And unless people start asking better questions—and demanding real accountability—they'll succeed.

**The Economic Cost of Ideology**

Ideology is expensive. Not in theory—in reality. And when ideological governance takes root at the top of a nation's financial, regulatory, and political institutions, the price isn't paid by the theorists or the policy designers. It's paid by the workers, the taxpayers, the savers, and the families who still believe that economics should be about efficiency, growth, and opportunity—not virtue signaling and social engineering.

Under Mark Carney's influence, and that of his globalist contemporaries, we've seen economics rebranded as a tool for enforcing morality—their morality. Whether through climate-linked finance, DEI quotas baked into central bank lending, or ESG mandates on pension funds, the core mission of capital—to be allocated to its most productive use—has been displaced by utopian agendas with little tolerance for dissent and even less room for economic pragmatism.

The result? Misallocated resources. Choked productivity. Artificial scarcity. Soaring inflation.

Let's call it what it is: ideological taxation.

When banks are punished for lending to fossil fuel producers—even in energy-starved economies—the result is not decarbonization. It's supply shocks, higher gas prices, and foreign dependence. When companies are judged not on profitability or innovation but on compliance with ESG metrics, the market stops rewarding excellence and starts rewarding ideological loyalty.

When every institutional decision must first pass through the filters of sustainability, equity, or inclusion, the result is not a fairer economy. It's a slower one. A costlier one. A less accountable one.

Carney doesn't hide this. He calls it a "values-based economy." What he leaves unsaid is that the values are imposed by unelected technocrats, administered through financial coercion, and enforced without recourse. This is economics stripped of its neutral character and converted into an instrument of behavioral control.

What's worse is the opportunity cost.

While countries like Canada and the UK are shackling their industries with ESG red tape and Net Zero compliance regimes, competitors like China, India, and the Gulf States are eating our lunch. They're building real infrastructure, producing energy, and securing rare earth supply chains—without pausing to ask if their investment strategy is "inclusive" enough.

This ideological cost isn't theoretical. It's measured in:

Manufacturing jobs lost.

Investment dollars fleeing overregulation.

Young families priced out of homes.

Retirees seeing their savings eroded.

Small businesses suffocated by compliance costs.

And every time a critic points this out, they're labeled as regressive, anti-science, or worse. But this isn't about being anti-future. It's about being pro-reality.

A reality where sound money matters. Where resource development is not a sin. Where free markets are allowed to price risk, not redistribute guilt.

The economic cost of ideology is not just rising. It's metastasizing. And unless we course-correct, we'll find ourselves in a world where we are poorer, colder, more dependent, and less free—all in the name of ideals that were never honestly debated, never democratically chosen, and never economically sound.

Carney's economic model demands sacrifice—but never from the top.

# Chapter 12: The Man, the Myth, the Model

Mark Carney is not just a man. He's a model—a prototype for a new breed of unelected ruler rising from the ashes of democratic decline. A technocrat cloaked in the language of sustainability. A financier recast as a moral authority. A bureaucrat elevated into a statesman without ever having to win a single vote.

In Carney, the global elite have found the perfect avatar: credentialed, connected, unflappable, and above reproach. He exudes calm while piloting chaos. He speaks in frameworks, not truths. He commands headlines without controversy, and policy influence without public mandate.

He is, in essence, the myth of competence personified—the trusted adult in the room while society collapses outside the window.

But beneath the smooth exterior lies the architecture of a deeper shift. Carney is not an outlier—he's the blueprint. A new form of power is being constructed around his image. It wears the garb of impartiality but serves a class agenda. It performs virtue but delivers consolidation. It promises resilience while producing compliance.

The myth is that this model is inevitable. That modern complexity requires a managerial priesthood of data wizards and systems integrators to steer society away from its own self-destructive tendencies. That elections are too messy. That markets are too wild. That freedom is too risky. So instead, we need calibrated governance by those who know best.

Carney fits this mold exactly. Trained at Harvard and Oxford. Forged in Goldman Sachs. Anointed by central banks. Celebrated by the WEF. Trusted by the UN. He's not just a man with experience—he's an embodiment of a worldview where policy is not debated but programmed.

The model he represents is built on several key tenets:

Technocratic infallibility – Decisions are best made by data and consensus, not by messy democratic processes.

Financial moralism – Markets are no longer neutral mechanisms of value exchange, but tools to correct human behavior.

Globalist uniformity – National sovereignty must yield to international coordination in climate, finance, and digital governance.

Public-private fusion – Institutions like Brookfield, the UN, and central banks blur the lines between corporate ambition and public interest.

In this model, leadership is no longer earned through service or tested in adversity. It is appointed from above, credentialed through networks, and sheltered from consequence. Accountability becomes performative. Power becomes abstract. And resistance becomes "disinformation."

Carney's myth—polished, intelligent, benevolent—is crucial to the survival of this model. He offers a face the public can trust while policies are implemented they'd never vote for. The carbon tax. The digital dollar. The ESG score. The post-growth economy. All quietly smuggled in under the banner of stability.

But stability for whom?

The myth only survives because the costs are invisible—spread across generations, currencies, and borders. Your purchasing power erodes, but the system remains intact. Your freedoms shrink, but your options expand in apps. Your leaders change, but your policies don't. That's the genius of the model. It is disguised permanence.

Carney may never become Prime Minister, and he may never need to. His influence is more potent where it can't be voted out. His policies live on in the framework, the boardroom, the bond markets, and the bureaucracies that now govern more than governments.

He is not just the man behind the curtain. He is the curtain.

And the longer we mistake the myth for merit, the more we enable the rise of an unaccountable class that speaks the language of virtue while building the scaffolding of control.

No elections, no dissent, no transparency—this is the quiet architecture of the new world order being prototyped in plain sight, and Mark Carney is one of its principal engineers.

Gone is the messy ritual of democratic choice. In its place: expert panels, stakeholder forums, ESG scorecards, and closed-door summits. Policies that shape your life are no longer debated in Parliament or Congress—they're hashed out between investment firms, central banks, and international NGOs. You don't vote on green bonds, carbon credits, or CBDCs. You inherit them.

Dissent is rebranded as extremism. Objection becomes misinformation. The terms are preloaded: if you question the system, you are either too ignorant to understand it or too dangerous to be heard. The managerial class, embodied by Carney, calls it resilience. But what they mean is compliance.

And transparency? Only for you. Your finances, habits, emissions, and "digital behavior" will be scrutinized, scored, and steered. But theirs—the meetings, the incentives, the offshore partnerships and revolving doors between government and mega-cap asset managers—remain hidden in the shadows.

This is the essence of the Carney doctrine. Not governance by consent, but governance by configuration—a system that no longer asks your permission, only your participation.

Voluntary, of course. Until it isn't.

What Mark Carney's career tells us about the future of power is simple: it's shifting upward, inward, and away from you.

Carney didn't climb through party politics. He didn't campaign. He didn't need to win the trust of voters. Instead, he ascended through a series of appointed positions—first in investment banking, then in the central banking world, and eventually into the international climate-industrial complex. Along the way, he perfected a new type of influence: technocratic, unaccountable, globalized.

This is the emerging model of power. It bypasses legislatures. It answers not to citizens, but to shareholders, intergovernmental bodies, and unelected boards. It speaks in acronyms—ESG, SDGs, CBDCs—but its language is control. Through financial systems, regulatory frameworks, and "climate finance," it builds a world where everything is measurable, tradeable, and programmable—including you.

Carney's career is a case study in how legacy institutions—from central banks to sovereign governments—are being retooled to serve a new elite consensus. One that speaks of equity while consolidating wealth. One that promises sustainability while designing scarcity. One that waves the flag of democracy while quietly dissolving its mechanisms.

He is not an outlier. He is the blueprint.

The future of power won't look like parliament—it will look like a boardroom. It won't sound like a political speech—it will sound like a quarterly report. And it won't be decided by ballots, but by backchannel consensus—until there's no meaningful opposition left to offer.

# 13

# Conclusion: Pulling Back the Curtain

**M**ark Carney is not an aberration—he's a blueprint
       To see Mark Carney clearly is to see the architecture of modern power. He did not stumble into influence, nor was he swept up by the tides of fate. He was cultivated—by institutions, by ideologies, and by a system that increasingly rewards obedience to supranational priorities over allegiance to the public good.

His career arc mirrors the shift from representative democracy to technocratic governance, from free-market capitalism to managed "stakeholder" economies, and from national sovereignty to global consensus enforcement. The man behind the green curtain is not just pushing policy—he's prototyping the next generation of global leadership: unelected, unaccountable, and insulated from public recourse.

In Carney's story, we see the erasure of meaningful democratic process—replaced by narrative management, ESG frameworks, and an economic priesthood that speaks in riddles about sustainability while drafting the rules of compliance behind closed doors.

He is not alone. His networks—Brookfield, Goldman Sachs, the Bank of England, the World Economic Forum, the UN—are not isolated islands. They are tentacles of a new machine, one that operates above the scrutiny of voters and beneath the radar of the mainstream.

This book has not argued that Carney is singularly responsible for the world we're inheriting. Instead, it has aimed to show how his journey illustrates the larger system of elite coordination that increasingly defines governance in the 21st century.

To pull back the curtain is not merely to expose a man, but a model. A model that must be understood if it is ever to be challenged.

Because if Mark Carney is the future, then the future is centralized, digitized, and deeply divorced from consent.

And if we do not draw that line now—if we do not name this blueprint for what it is—then the window to course correct will close.

Not with a bang. But with a quiet agreement. Signed in a boardroom. Drafted in Davos. Endorsed by no one you elected.

## How Citizens Can Recognize the Real Agendas Behind the Curtain

If the past few decades have taught us anything, it's that the surface story is rarely the real story. The press conferences, talking points, and glossy sustainability reports are often the packaging for agendas that serve power—not people. Learning to recognize what lies beneath that surface is no longer a luxury; it's a civic imperative.

Here are key ways citizens can pull back the curtain for themselves:

1. Follow the money—not the mission.

When a banker, bureaucrat, or billionaire speaks of equity, sustainability, or justice, ask: Who benefits financially? ESG sounds noble, but when trillions of dollars flow into it through private capital while citizens foot the inflation bill, the green mask starts to slip. Look not at what they say, but at where the capital consolidates.

2. Watch the language shift.

New power doesn't arrive with tanks—it arrives with rebranded terminology. "Stakeholder capitalism," "build back better," "inclusive growth," "Net Zero"—these aren't ideologies; they're compliance frameworks dressed as virtue. Pay attention to buzzwords that avoid specificity while signaling broad agreement. Real reform doesn't need a branding agency.

3. Ask who wasn't at the table.

Most sweeping changes today—whether in finance, climate, health, or digital policy—are made without referendums, without legislative debate, and without public scrutiny. If the decision affects everyone but was made by a select few at Davos, in central banks, or behind the closed doors of international summits, it isn't governance—it's orchestration.

4. Study affiliations, not resumes.

Carney is not just "former Bank of Canada and Bank of England governor"—he's a product of Goldman Sachs, Brookfield, the WEF, and the UN. These are not neutral institutions. They form an ecosystem of global influence that speaks in the same accent and operates with the same assumptions: that markets, not people, should shape the future.

5. Note the revolving doors.

Pay attention to who moves from politics to finance to international NGOs and back again. When the same individual can be a central banker, a private equity executive, and a climate envoy within five years, we're no longer dealing with distinct roles. We're dealing with a class—interchangeable, insulated, and above democratic reproach.

6. Look for what's being centralized.

CBDCs, digital ID systems, ESG-linked banking, and global regulatory alignment all have one thing in common: they consolidate control. If a policy proposal results in fewer levers of power being in your hands and more in an unaccountable network's grip, it's not about innovation—it's about enclosure.

7. Trust the unpopular questions.

Real journalism and real inquiry often begin where the press releases stop. If someone is being deplatformed, censored, or mocked for asking about conflicts of interest, financial collusion, or sovereignty, don't dismiss them—listen more closely. Disinformation is often a label applied to uncomfortable truths.

8. Demand consent, not just consensus.

A WEF panel agreeing that citizens need to "own nothing" is not consent. A U.N. envoy deciding carbon targets for your farm is not consent. A private bank linking your mortgage to your climate behavior is not consent. If your voice wasn't part of the decision, you are the subject—not the beneficiary—of that decision.

9. Reject the manufactured crises.

The "climate emergency," "pandemic preparedness," and "digital threats" are all real concerns—but they've also been weaponized as justifications for sweeping new powers. Crises now function as delivery vehicles for control systems. Ask not just what's happening, but what's being allowed to happen because of it.

10. Reclaim local reality.

The antidote to globalist abstraction is local accountability. Know your mayor, support independent journalism, build parallel economies, share this knowledge. The more decentralized your information, income, and influence become, the less vulnerable you are to the mandates of international bureaucracies you never elected.

Citizenship in the 21st century requires discernment.

The curtain has not been fully drawn, but the seams are showing. The sooner we learn to read through the press releases, decode the initiatives, and name the unelected hands behind the policies, the more equipped we'll be to resist their quiet takeover.

This isn't conspiracy. It's comprehension.

And it starts with seeing clearly—and refusing to look away.

**Sovereignty vs. Submission in the Age of Technocracy**

In past eras, sovereignty was an overt contest—crowns and empires, charters and revolutions, flags raised and borders drawn. But in the 21st century, sovereignty is not surrendered on the battlefield. It is ceded silently, in trade agreements, digital standards, ESG mandates, and unaccountable global compacts. It is not seized—it is signed away.

Technocracy doesn't march. It measures.

It doesn't ask for allegiance. It programs it.

The age of technocracy redefines governance as expertise, replaces representation with credentialism, and masks submission as convenience. No longer do you need to kneel to the king. The algorithm already knows what you want. You need only comply.

Mark Carney's rise is emblematic of this transformation. He didn't take power—he became the administrator of systems that operate above it. The World Economic Forum calls it "public-private cooperation." In truth, it is public surrender and private rule.

Under technocracy, sovereignty becomes obsolete—not because it has failed, but because it has become inconvenient to the aims of those who see national boundaries, democratic processes, and local cultures as friction points in the architecture of global management.

This is not globalization. It is homogenization.

The sovereign individual becomes a "user." The sovereign nation becomes a "stakeholder." The sovereign vote becomes a metric to be nudged. "Social license," not civil liberty, becomes the moral currency. And those who question the process? They're labeled deniers, extremists, or noncompliant—not citizens.

Carney's role in this system is not as tyrant but as template. His financial diplomacy, ESG activism, and climate evangelism are not personal ambitions—they are the playbook. He is the bridge between governments that pretend to serve and corporations that actually rule.

In the age of technocracy, submission is not enforced—it is automated. Central bank digital currencies linked to social metrics. Climate mandates tied to housing and transportation. "One Health" policies that erase medical freedom. The citizen is invited to participate only after the code has been written, the framework funded, the options narrowed.

Sovereignty, in this climate, becomes an act of rebellion.

To remain sovereign is to refuse the false binaries. To reject the choice between corporate capture and centralized command. To demand that the human soul not be reduced to a behavioral statistic, a carbon output, or a risk factor in someone else's model.

Sovereignty means saying no to digital leashes disguised as progress.

It means refusing to be nudged, scored, and shaped by systems that were not born from your culture, your vote, or your consent.

It means restoring the sacred truth that no credential, title, or simulation replaces the right of a people to govern themselves—or of a man to own his life.

Technocracy doesn't end in jackboots. It ends in submission by software.

And sovereignty begins where you choose not to update.

# 14

# Timeline: Carney's Career and Key Appointments

1<sup>965</sup>

1 965
Birth: Born March 16, 1965, in Fort Smith, Northwest Territories, Canada.

1970s–1980s

Raised in Edmonton, Alberta.

Attended St. Francis Xavier High School.

Early interest in public affairs; father a high school principal and left-leaning academic.

1988

Graduates from Harvard University with a bachelor's degree in economics.

Works briefly for the Canadian Department of Finance.

1990–1995

Earns an MPhil (1993) and DPhil (1995) in Economics at the University of Oxford (St. Peter's College, later Nuffield).

Thesis on the dynamic macroeconomic effects of fiscal policy.

1995–2003

Joins Goldman Sachs.

Spends over a decade in London, New York, Toronto, and Tokyo.

Specializes in sovereign risk and emerging markets.

2003

Returns to Canada.

Appointed Deputy Governor of the Bank of Canada under David Dodge.

2004–2007

Moves to the Department of Finance Canada as Senior Associate Deputy Minister.

Key adviser to then-Finance Minister Jim Flaherty.

Helps steer fiscal policy during pre-2008 financial concerns.

2008–2013

Appointed Governor of the Bank of Canada (February 1, 2008 – June 1, 2013).

Oversees Canadian monetary policy during the Global Financial Crisis.

Gains international praise for Canada's relative stability.

Chairs the Financial Stability Board's Standing Committee on Supervisory and Regulatory Cooperation (2009–2011).

2011–2018

Chair of the Financial Stability Board (FSB), appointed by G20 leaders.

Promotes global regulatory reforms and banking oversight.

2013–2020

Governor of the Bank of England (July 1, 2013 – March 15, 2020).

First non-British national in the role.

Manages financial policy during Brexit and turbulent EU negotiations.

Introduces controversial stances on climate change and inequality.

2020

Appointed UN Special Envoy for Climate Action and Finance by UN Secretary-General António Guterres (December 2019 announcement, formalized in 2020).

Begins using global platform to promote ESG, sustainable investing, and carbon credits.

2020–2025

Vice Chair and Head of ESG and Impact Investing at Brookfield Asset Management.

Becomes Chair of Brookfield Asset Management following the 2022 spin-off of its asset management business.

Plays key role in their $15B net-zero Transition Fund.

2021–Present

Member of the King's Privy Council for Canada, appointed quietly under the Trudeau government.

Continues as a public speaker, author (Values: Building a Better World for All), and advocate for climate finance reform.

Tipped as a future Liberal Party leader or Prime Ministerial candidate.

# 15

# References and Source Documentation

Bank of Canada. (2007). Mark Carney appointed Governor of the Bank of Canada. Retrieved from https://www.bankofcanada.ca/2007/10/mark-carney-appointed-governor-bank-canada/

Bank of Canada. (n.d.). Mark Carney – Biography. Retrieved from https://www.bankofcanada.ca/profile/mark-carney/

Bank of England. (n.d.). Mark Carney biography. Retrieved from https://www.bankofengland.co.uk/about/people/past/mark-carney/biography

Bank of England. (2019). Mark Carney named United Nations Special Envoy for Climate Action and Finance. Retrieved from https://www.bankofengland.co.uk/news/2019/december/mark-carney-named-united-nations-special-envoy-for-climate-action-and-finance

BNN Bloomberg. (2022). Mark Carney to chair Brookfield Asset Management post-spin out. Retrieved from https://www.bnnbloomberg.ca/mark-carney-to-chair-brookfield-asset-management-post-spin-out-1.1816977

Brookfield. (2020). Brookfield announces appointment of Mark Carney as Vice Chair and Head of ESG and Impact Fund Investing. Retrieved from https://bn.brookfield.com/press-releases/brookfield-announces-appointment-mark-carney-vice-chair-and-head-esg-and-impact-fund

Canadian Encyclopedia. (n.d.). Mark Carney. Retrieved from https://www.thecanadianencyclopedia.ca/en/article/mark-carney

Forbes. (2024). Canada's New PM, Mark Carney: Pro-CBDC, Anti-Decentralization. Retrieved from https://www.forbes.com/

Government of Canada. (n.d.). King's Privy Council for Canada. Retrieved from https://www.canada.ca/en/privy-council.html

Jacobin Magazine. (2023). Canada is betting on Mark Carney, technocrat extraordinaire. Retrieved from https://jacobin.com/

Ledger Insights. (2020). Mark Carney: stablecoins should have access to central bank balance sheet. Retrieved from https://www.ledgerinsights.com/mark-carney-stablecoins-central-bank/

Project Syndicate. (2020). Schwab, K. What Kind of Capitalism Do We Want? Retrieved from https://www.project-syndicate.org/commentary/klaus-schwab-stakeholder-capitalism-by-klaus-schwab-2020-01

Reuters. (2022). Mark Carney to chair Brookfield Asset Management. Retrieved from https://www.reuters.com/business/finance/mark-carney-chair-brookfield-asset-management-post-spin-out-2022-08-11/

United Nations. (2019). Secretary-General Appoints Mark Joseph Carney of Canada as Special Envoy on Climate Action and Finance. Retrieved from https://press.un.org/en/2019/sga1927.doc.htm

Wikipedia. (n.d.). Mark Carney. Retrieved from https://en.wikipedia.org/wiki/Mark_Carney

World Economic Forum. (2021). Measuring Stakeholder Capitalism: Towards Common Metrics. Retrieved from https://www.weforum.org/reports/measuring-stakeholder-capitalism/

www.ingramcontent.com/pod-product-compliance
Lightning Source LLC
Chambersburg PA
CBHW071536120626
46550CB00006B/2477